Richard Henry Dana, Sr.

Twayne's United States Authors Series

Lewis Leary, Editor

University of North Carolina at Chapel Hill

TUSAS 511

RICHARD HENRY DANA, SR.
(1787–1879)
Photograph courtesy of Longfellow National
Historic Site, Cambridge, Massachusetts

Richard Henry Dana, Sr.

By Doreen M. Hunter

Fort Lewis College

Twayne Publishers
A Division of G.K. Hall. & Co. • Boston

Richard Henry Dana, Sr.

Doreen M. Hunter

Copyediting supervised by Lewis DeSimone
Book design by Barbara Anderson

Typeset in 11 pt. Garamond
by P&M Typesetting, Waterbury, Connecticut

Printed on permanent/durable acid-free paper
and bound in the United State of America

Library of Congress Cataloging-in-Publication Data

Hunter, Doreen M.
    Richard Henry Dana, Sr.

    (Twayne's United States authors series ; TUSAS 511)
    Bibliography
    Includes index.
    1. Dana, Richard Henry, 1787–1879—Criticism and
interpretation.   I. Title.   II. Series.
PS1502.H86   1987   818'.209   86-22891
ISBN 0-8057-7490-4

Contents

About the Author

Doreen Hunter grew up in Walla Walla, Washington, and received her B.A. from Stanford University and her Ph.D. from the University of California at Berkeley. She has published articles on aspects of nineteenth-century American thought in *New England Quarterly, American Studies,* and *American Quarterly.* She has taught at the University of East Anglia in Norwich, England, and Virginia Tech, and is presently teaching American history at Fort Lewis College in Durango, Colorado.

Preface

Richard Henry Dana, Sr. (1787–1879) was a poet, literary critic, essayist, and writer of short fiction. He was born too late to find inspiration in the promise and turmoil of the Revolution but too soon to escape the uncertainties that troubled writers and artists before the American Renaissance. Although less well known and less talented than his contemporaries—Irving, Cooper, and Bryant—he recognized with greater clarity the inadequacies of eighteenth-century rationalism and the exhaustion of the possibilities of literary neoclassicism. His claim to the attention of modern readers rests on the fact that he was a pioneering figure in the romantic movement in America. Though not the first American to write about nature in the romantic vein (that distinction probably belongs to Philip Freneau), he was the first to grapple in a serious way with the philosophical and literary implications of the romantic vision.

During the twenty years of his active writing career, Dana explored the various possibilities of romanticism. Starting out as a disciple of Wordsworth and Coleridge, he wrote critical reviews that celebrated the spiritual suggestiveness of nature and the creative, godlike powers of the imagination. After a period of grief and near madness, however, his faith in the imagination as a redemptive source of spiritual truth was shattered. He became convinced that the imagination has no necessary connection with a transcendent reality but instead arises from the subjective, unconscious, and possibly dangerous part of the human mind. He sought refuge from this bleak nihilism in orthodox Christianity, but his pilgrimage did not end there. Although worn out by poor health, poverty, and the overwhelmingly negative reaction to his work—not just the hostility of critics but also the indignant incomprehension of the reading public—he went on to give forceful expression to a romantic cultural critique. Not content with clichés about the materialism and practicality of Americans, he identified what he believed were the more serious causes of the nation's cultural shallowness—the homogenizing effects of democracy, a contempt for the past, and the prudery and anti-intellectualism encouraged by religious sects.

Dana's career provides a unique vantage point from which to view the transition in American thought from the Enlightenment to the romantic movement. Unlike some other American romanticists whose limited literary talents bound them to the superficial mannerisms of the movement, Dana seems to have been freed by his limitations to wrestle with the deeper ethical, aesthetic, and philosophical implications of these new ideas. Had his literary gifts been more impressive, had his imagination been more fertile, and had his ability to embody complex ideas in convincing dramatic forms been more commanding, he might well have paused to mine his talents. As it was, he scouted the implications of romanticism with a revealing perceptivity and directness.

In his own day, a few of his younger contemporaries—Fuller, Poe, and Alcott, for example—expressed admiration for his intelligence, his terse masculine style, and his determination to treat ambitious and difficult themes; but he exerted no direct influence on later writers. Indeed, to them he represented the fevered sensibility and palsied will that they wished most to avoid. Today we cannot read his stories and poems with much pleasure. Nevertheless, to neglect his work entirely is to risk impoverishing our understanding of romanticism and of the literary life in America in the early nineteenth century. Every important literary movement has its pioneers, consisting essentially of lonely and isolated men who protest the conventions and half-truths of the old order. Although they may fail to produce work of great literary merit, they pose the issues and conduct the experiments in style and form that will engage the writers of the next generation. Dana was such a pioneer. His story is worth hearing because it offers us insight into the influences that shaped romanticism in America and into the hostile cultural environment in which romantic ideas had to make their way. It is also worth attention because Dana, in his own right, was an intelligent man whose efforts to validate an idealistic explanation of human experience led him to explore the psychological labyrinths unlocked by the romantic movement. Whether the psychological tales of Poe or Hawthorne, the metaphysical novels of Melville, or the transcendental musings of Emerson, there is no expression of the romantic literary movement that Richard Henry Dana, Sr., did not in some way anticipate.

Doreen M. Hunter

Fort Lewis College

Acknowledgments

I was granted permission to publish manuscript material through the courtesy of the Trustees of the Boston Public Library, the Massachusetts Historical Society, and the Rare Books and Manuscripts Division of the New York Public Library, Astor, Lenox and Tilden Foundations. Material from the Alcott-Pratt manuscripts has been published by permission of Houghton Library. The Longfellow National Historic Site granted me permission to publish the reproduction of the photograph of Richard Henry Dana, Sr. I also wish to acknowledge the encouragement and generosity of my friend and colleague Eleanor Lyons whose careful and knowledgeable reading of the manuscript saved me from untold errors and infelicities.

Chronology

1787   Richard Henry Dana, Sr., born 15 November to Elizabeth Ellery and Francis Dana, fifth of five children.

1797   Sent to school in Newport, Rhode Island.

1804   Enters Harvard College. Brother Francis's speculations fail, greatly diminishing the family's fortune.

1807   Expelled from Harvard for participating in the Rotten Cabbage Rebellion. Death of his mother.

1809   Begins the study of law in the offices of his cousin Francis Dana Channing.

1811   Death of his father, Judge Francis Dana.

1812   Admitted to the bar and begins the practice of law in Sutton, Massachusetts.

1813   Marries Ruth Charlotte Smith of Providence, Rhode Island. (The couple had four children: Richard Henry Dana, Jr., Ruth Charlotte Dana, Edmund "Ned" Trowbridge Dana, and Susan Dana.)

1815   Founding of the original *North American Review.*

1818   Named assistant editor for the *North American Review,* which publishes his important essay on William Hazlitt's *Lectures on the English Poets.*

1819   Denied the editorship of the *North American Review.*

1821   Publishes the first issue of the *Idle Man.*

1822   Death of his wife, Ruth Charlotte, and infant daughter Susan. Ceases publishing the *Idle Man* with the issue containing the controversial story "Paul Felton."

1826   Converted to Congregationalism during the revivals of Lyman Beecher.

1827   Publishes *The Buccaneer and Other Poems.* Involved in the controversy between Congregationalists and Unitarians in his parish in Cambridge.

1830   Analyzes the religious culture of his day in his review article of Taylor's *National History of Enthusiasm,* published in the May issue of the *Spirit of the Pilgrims.*

1833   Publishes collected edition of his stories and poems, *Poems and Prose Writings.*

1834   Gives Fourth of July oration on "The Law as Suited to Man."

1835   Begins classes for women on English literature.

1838   Lectures on Shakespeare in Providence, Rhode Island.

1843   Confirmed in St. Paul's Episcopal Church of Boston. Death of Washington Allston.

1844   Is one of founders of the Church of the Advent.

1849   Gives highly successful lecture series in Philadelphia.

1850   Publishes second edition of *Poems and Prose Writings.* Conducts last of his lecture tours.

1879   Dies 2 February.

Chapter One
The Ambiguous Heritage
The Danas of Boston

Distinguished ancestors can be a source of both pride and anxiety. Although the wealth and status associated with their names may clear the way to opportunity, their legacy can also saddle descendants with expectations and views of life that are inappropriate in a later age. For those who come after, the humiliation of failure can be sharper, the fear of inadequacy more paralyzing. The life of Richard Henry Dana, Sr., was tormented by such an ambiguous heritage.

For four generations, his ancestors had played influential roles in the cultural, commercial, and political life of Massachusetts. The first Richard Dana arrived in the colony in 1640. Starting as a day laborer mowing hay along the Charles River, he prospered and acquired land, political office, and a large family of ten children. Dana's paternal grandfather, also named Richard, was a Harvard graduate (class of 1718) and an outstanding attorney. Through marriage to Lydia Trowbridge, the sister of Massachusetts Attorney General Edmund Trowbridge, he substantially increased the family fortune. He joined the Sons of Liberty, a movement organized to resist, by violent means if necessary, the new revenue acts imposed on the colonies by England, and he became an influential spokesman for the patriot cause until his death in 1772.

On his mother's side, Dana was a descendant of the poet Anne Bradstreet. His maternal grandfather was William Ellery, a wealthy merchant of Newport, Rhode Island. He too was an ardent patriot, one of the Sons of Liberty who led the citizens of Newport in a riot against the Stamp Act. He served in the Continental Congress and in the Rhode Island Constitutional ratifying convention, during which, obedient to the instructions of his independently minded constituents, he opposed the new Constitution. In 1790 he was appointed as the Newport collector of customs, a post he held until his death in 1820 at the age of ninety-three.

His father, Francis Dana, was a High Federalist whose zeal for national independence was greater than his enthusiasm for the republican experiment that followed. Like his father before him, he became a lawyer and enhanced the family's position by marrying Elizabeth Ellery. He joined the Sons of Liberty and was elected to the Continental Congress in 1776. During the Revolution, he served as secretary to the American legation in France and as an unrecognized envoy to the court of Catherine II of Russia. In 1785 he was appointed to the Massachusetts Supreme Court, becoming the chief justice in 1791. Convinced that the courts must serve as a bulwark against the popular democratic currents of the day, he gained notoriety in the state by haranguing juries on the conservative principles of Federalist political philosophy. Proud, stern, high-strung, and increasingly morose, he deplored the fact that the people of Massachusetts deferred less and less to the opinions of men of his social rank. Francis Dana honored the style of the eighteenth century in his dress and manners as well as in his politics. He offended his fellow citizens by riding circuit in "the style of an English lord."[1] Accompanied by liverymen and carrying a gold-headed cane, he arrived at court each day in a carriage bearing the family coat of arms.

Richard Henry Dana, Sr., was born on 15 November 1787, the youngest of Judge Dana's five children. He had a lonely, gloomy childhood. In later years he rarely mentioned his boyhood but hinted at its emotional austerity in his fiction, where parental figures are depicted as remote, ineffectual, and preoccupied with grief and worldly reversals. His mother's poor health and his father's busy and controversial legal career left them little time to devote to their youngest son. Neither his sister Martha, who assumed much of the responsibility for his care, nor his brother Edmund, who inspired his boyish admiration, was close enough in age to break through the young Dana's solitude.

His happiest memories were associated with the years he spent in the home of his grandfather, William Ellery, to whom he was sent at the age of ten in order to attend school in Newport. In the companionship of his cousins and his grandfather, Dana found the affection and the cheerful atmosphere he missed in his own home. By all accounts, Ellery was a remarkable man and played a decisive role in the upbringing of several of Massachusetts's more distinguished leaders. He was a surrogate father not only to Dana but also to his widowed daughter Lucy's nine children, including the Unitarian minister William Ellery Channing, the physician Walter Channing, and the Harvard professor of rhetoric Edward Tyrell Channing. Ellery took a genuine interest in the moral and intellectual development of his grandsons, and they, in turn, admired and revered him. Edward Tyrell Channing recalled that they were drawn to him "as if he were their dependence; and they felt that they owed to him, not only some of their best remembered seasons of pleasure, but in no small degree, the direction and colouring of their thoughts. . . . In any new train of reflection, which they could not possibly trace to him, his image was likely to be revived, his probable view of the subject to be suggested, his provoking objections, his moderate approval, his pretended misconception, and his sincere interest. He was not their teacher, but their elder companion."[2] Ellery "would do what he could to keep company with them, and encourage them to talk about anything that occupied them, and to invite them in their turn to enter with him in his own favorite inquiries, so that nothing should separate them or weaken their intimacy."[3]

Because his father was such a distant figure, Dana relied on his grandfather for affection, guidance, and encouragement. Ellery, whose literary interests favored the classics and Queen Anne poets, inspired in his grandson a deep love of philosophy and English literature. He encouraged the boy to read and to think for himself, assuring him that he possessed a "sound and discriminating mind." Although sympathetic with Dana's diffident, shy, and sensitive personality, Ellery feared that self-doubt and an apparent lack of ambition would destroy the boy's chances of success. He urged Dana to accept the obligations and responsibilities of men of their class and station. For years Dana looked upon his grandfather as his chief friend and confidant. Later, when things went hard with him and he felt compelled to make choices that disappointed the hopes of his family, including Ellery, he knew that he could always count on his grandfather for understanding and support.

At Harvard, which he entered in 1804, Dana's uncertainty about his future and his vague discontent with the conventional wisdom of his day grew more intense. The college had become a stronghold of the moderate American Enlightenment. The philosophical ideas of John Locke and of his revisionist defenders, the Scottish commonsense realists, were spread throughout the curriculum. The Scots—Thomas Reid, Dugald Stewart, Thomas Brown—had set out to bolster Locke's theory of knowledge against David Hume's skepticism and

George Berkeley's metaphysical idealism. The Scots reassured those interested in such abstruse questions that any uncertainty about the identity between ideas or sensations and the actual objects that give rise to these sensations was unnecessary. According to the Scots, the world exists and our experience of it is reliable. The common sense of humankind is adequate for all purposes of life. The position of the Scots cannot, of course, be treated adequately in a few sentences: their ideas were more diverse and sophisticated than these remarks suggest. Nevertheless, when translated into the homilies of the pulpit and the classroom, their ideas provided reassuring support for traditional beliefs. The president of Harvard, Samuel Webber, and the new professor of divinity, Henry Ware, Sr., encouraged an integration of Scottish commonsense realism and Unitarian Christianity, which dominated Harvard for over half a century. In chapel they taught that religious belief was perfectly consistent with reason and empirical evidence. Dana's teachers conveyed a mechanistic Newtonian view of the universe, confidently assuring students that nature was so rationally ordered that science would master all its secrets in time. Students were told that in this rational clockwork universe, the virtues most usefully cultivated were moderation and good sense. They were advised to cherish delicate and refined feelings but to suppress passion, to seek out universal truths but to avoid the individual and the exceptional.

Although Dana's professors were well-intentioned men, their methods would have wilted the interest of any spirited youth. They gave neither instructions nor explanations but listened to recitations and recorded marks signifying each student's ability to memorize assigned materials. Under this intellectually numbing system, Dana studied classical languages, classical literature, Hebrew, French, arithmetic, algebra, trigonometry, composition, history, and logic. His instructor in logic, Levi Hedge, was a follower of the Scottish philosopher Thomas Brown. He was an exacting, pedantic man remembered by several generations of Harvard graduates for forcing his students to recite verbatim the textbook he had written.[4] Although scholars have testified to the merits of Hedge's *Elements of Logick,* Dana remembered his course with unqualified distaste. His whole being revolted against the psychological theories of Locke, upon which Hedge based his *Logick.* Hedge's detailed analysis of the operations of the mind seemed to reduce all mental processes to the predictable functioning of a machine. Passion, imagination, intuition—all the manifestations of the mind that might absorb the interests of a young and intellectually restless undergraduate—were largely ignored. By treating philosophy as a branch of science, by restricting inquiry to questions about the gathering and processing of information, Locke and Hedge neglected those questions of ethics, metaphysics, and aesthetics that most interested Dana. Many years later, Dana explained to a friend how his course at Harvard had robbed him of his true calling:

That I have a preference for the Poetic form of philosophy is perhaps true; but next to this is philosophy as it shows itself in the "Speculative Intellect." Had there been a Coleridge when I was a boy, I should have been deep in for it. But there was Locke on the *Understanding* put before my eyes; & the atmosphere about me was the spirit of Locke,—an atmosphere which I could not breathe in—so rare, so cold. Add to this, the teacher of Locke was Prof. Hedge. I was too young to see where the defect lay; but my consciousness (shall I call it?) satisfied me that there was a radical defect. The more I read, the more I felt the want of something. Could a hog, when his viscera have been appropriated for a harslet dinner & stuffed sausages, be endowed with sensation, in his empty condition, he would feel much as I used to feel after reading Locke. Thus you see how I was kept from being a prodigious philosopher, & led to writing reviews, & tales, & verses. [5]

To Dana the empirical approach of Locke and Hedge seemed to divert attention from the more speculative branches of philosophy. Taught that man cannot know the ultimate nature of things, urged to place confidence in the commonsense inductions and ordinary convictions born of everyday experience, he concluded that philosophy was less interesting and offered less insight into the mysteries of human nature and the universe than poetry.

His student days at Harvard ended appropriately when, in 1807, he was expelled for participating in a dining hall food riot known as the Rotten Cabbage Rebellion. It is tempting to think of his part in the riot as an expression of a deeper disgust with the educational fare. Tainted by officious rules, mindless methods of instruction, and philosophical ideas that conflicted with his emotional nature and meditative disposition, his education incited intellectual rebellion. His brother Edmund, who was eight years his senior, provided him with an unofficial curriculum and the encouragement for such defiance.

The Monthly Anthology Society

While Dana was attending Harvard, his brother Edmund and several friends were promoting preromantic ideas in the pages of a literary journal called the *Monthly Anthology*. Their enthusiasm for genius and untamed nature, and their appeals for a new poetry and a new style of literary criticism heightened Dana's dissatisfaction with instruction at Harvard. A career in the law, which he was expected to pursue, paled before his brother's accounts of the camaraderie and excitement of the literary life. Although his connection with the Monthly Anthology Society was the informal, secondhand, and idealized one provided by Edmund, it introduced him to the ideas that would in a few years lead him to romanticism. The controversies that his brother and friends waged with the more conservative members of the society created the context in which he tested his literary loyalties and began to fashion his own critical standards.

Edmund's desire to challenge the complacencies of the eighteenth century was nourished by friendships he formed at Harvard just before the turn of the century. As undergraduates, Edmund, Washington Allston, and Arthur Maynard Walter had been caught up in a mutinous mood. They were party to the rebellion that flickered on exhibition days at Harvard when students startled their instructors by praising the superiority of poetic genius and by questioning the brilliance and originality of the English demigods Newton and Locke.[6] In Allston's rooms off Harvard Yard, they gathered to share their enthusiasm for the exotic poetry of Robert Southey, the Gothic tales of Anne Radcliffe, and the Sturm und Drang plays of Friedrich von Schiller.[7] They delighted in the foreign settings, the emotional extremes, and the defiance of bourgeois conventions depicted in this proscribed literature. They sensed the inadequacy of Locke's psychology for understanding the diversity of the individual's spiritual and emotional life. Edmund's unhappiness with the educational system at Harvard was so strong that he either quit or was expelled at the end of his third year.

Eager to rid themselves of their cultural provincialism, the three friends made plans to tour Europe together. Allston sailed for England in 1801 to study painting with Benjamin West. He was joined a year later by Dana and Walter. Over the next two years, they visited art galleries and theaters together and deepened their appreciation of European culture. They probably gained some insight into the intellectual currents that were carrying artists and writers away from the aesthetic and metaphysical ideas of the eighteenth century. (Already in Allston's paintings the topographical precision of the formalized landscape popular in the eighteenth century, was giving way to the imaginary landscape of reverie). Dana and Walter returned from Europe in 1804 with a strengthened resolve to help Americans shake off the fetters of the Enlightenment.

They got their chance when invited to join the Monthly Anthology Society, an association of young professional men of Boston. Membership included William Emerson (the father of Ralph Waldo Emerson), John Sylvester John Gardiner, Samuel Cooper Thacher, Joseph Stevens Buckminster (minister of the Brattle Street Church), John Kirkland (a future president of Harvard College), Dana, and Walter. Educated at Harvard and raised in the conservative political traditions of the Federalist party, these men wanted to seize the campaign for a national literature from the hands of the democratically minded supporters of Jefferson. They were afraid that egalitarianism, factionalism, and love of luxury were destroying the foundations of Christian morality and true learning. Convinced that great literature was dependent on good government and good morals, they thought of their journal as a weapon in the Federalist effort to restore virtue, order, and decorum in the American republic. Through the *Monthly Anthology,* which they modeled on the leading British journals of the day, they hoped to sponsor a national literature of distinction.

Tensions and disagreements lurked below the surface of consensus, however. Although Dana and Walter shared this Federalist political outlook, they disagreed with many members of the society over what constituted good literature. Those with a more traditional literary outlook cherished ideals and values borrowed from England's Augustan Age. They admired refinement of style, moderation and decorum in conduct, and had a taste for Latinate language and syntax. Their favorite writers were Pope, Johnson, Goldsmith, Steele, and Addison, men who self-consciously emulated the style of Roman writers in the Age of Augustus. Dana and Walter, on the other hand, preferred the new poetry and literature of the Age of Sensibility in England. They loved the wisdom of the heart above the calculations of the head and valued energy and passion above decorum and deference to tradition. Brought to the brink of romanticism by their enthusiasm for Gothic themes and for the lyric poetry of William Cowper and Thomas Gray, they praised literature that sought to convey the poet's private states of mind. It is not surprising that, divided by such differences in taste, the society members could not agree upon a strategy for encouraging a national literature. Some urged the literary values and practices of neoclassicism while others argued for the newer aesthetic ideas. Lewis P. Simpson, historian of the Monthly Anthology Society, summarizes the anthologists' dilemma: "The *Anthology* and Anthology society existed in a state of tension between a search after the illusory security, symbolized by the devotion to the image of the Augustan Age, and a hesitant awakening to new intellectual and spiritual forces."[8] This conflict was a harbinger of cultural tensions that persisted through the first half of the nineteenth century. It anticipated Richard Henry Dana's dispute with the editors of the *North American Review,* Ralph Waldo Emerson's with the Unitarians, and Herman Melville's with critics who thought *Moby Dick* an example of "bedlam literature."

Whether society members took their inspiration from Augustan writers or from the poets of the Age of Sensibility depended on their understanding of the meaning and significance of nature. They had all been trained in the empirical tradition of Lockean psychology and so believed that knowledge consists of reflections upon sensory data. Because nature embraces all that can be known by way of the senses, they believed that nature provides the model from which men may infer rules governing what is aesthetically pleasing, morally correct, and politically sound. The anthologists did not understand nature in the same way, however. They did not mean the same thing when they invoked nature as the standard for judging works of literature and the acts of individuals.

For conservatives like John Gardiner, John Kirkland, and Theodore Dehon, *nature* meant human nature, not the physical world of woods, lakes, mountains, and prairies. The term implied those qualities of moral and intellectual experience that were thought to be universal, unchanging, and therefore natural. They worshiped the God of Newton, that supreme craftsmen who governed the world according to elegant and precise mathematical laws. They admired the physical world around them because they saw in it an order and symmetry suggestive of the rational principles by which that God governed his creation.

The conservatives believed that this rational order of things was threatened by the spirit of innovation unleashed by the American Revolution. Like the eighteenth-century writers they admired, these

Augustans felt besieged on every side by rude and unwashed pretenders to learning and status. When they reviewed the achievements of the writers of the revolutionary generation, men like Joel Barlow, Philip Freneau, and Noah Webster, they reported a vista that was "all desert, a wide African sand garden, showing brambles, and rushes and weeds."[9] Nothing so aroused their indignation as the cult of the untutored genius. For this populist folly, they blamed revolutionary ideology, with its emphasis on the truths accessible to the unaided reason of ordinary people. To value originality, energy, and passion above obedience to established rules and models struck them as madness. Convinced that democracy bred a spirit fatal to literature and learning, the conservatives pleaded for a strengthing of classical studies, a renewed respect for eighteenth-century models of composition, and, on the part of aspiring writers, a cultivated indifference to the siren calls of popularity and political influence.

Joseph Stevens Buckminster occupied a middle position, sharing with the conservatives their respect for the classics and with the "radicals" their enthusiasm for poets of the Age of Sensibility. His response to nature was more subjective than the conservative's. Unlike Gardiner, for example, who believed that poets should reproduce with painterly exactness the beauty that objectively exists in things around them, Buckminster felt that the purpose of all art was to reproduce for others the effect of beauty on the artist's own mind. His aesthetic theories had been influenced by the British philosopher Edmund Burke, whose theory of the sublime emphasized qualities in nature—terror, obscurity, vastness, magnificence, and power—that have no exact visual equivalent. The inwardness and subjectivity of such experiences appealed to Buckminster, but seemed to invite a false and morally dangerous misrepresentation of the real world to the more traditional members of the society.

The argument between Gardiner and Buckminster over the lyric poetry of Thomas Gray reveals the nature of this breach over aesthetics. When Buckminster praised Gray's poetry for its originality, Gardiner spluttered, "Originality! Fiddledy-diddledy." To Gardiner's complaint that the poetry was obscure, Buckminster replied, "There is a higher species of poetry than the mere language of reason," adding that there were other ways of writing poetry than Pope's.[10] Buckminster valued truth to feeling above clarity and elegance. Addressing himself specifically to Gardiner's belief that beauty in art must be a faithful imitation of life, he observed that the "glow" of Gray's poetry "seems to consist in a certain felicity of terms, fraught with pictures, which it is impossible to transfer with perfect exactness to the canvas."[11]

Buckminster and his friend Samuel Thacher were more optimistic about the future of a national literature than many conservatives. Because the American landscape offered so many examples of the sublime and because its novel appearance offered no excuse for endless copies of "the lilies and roses of Europe, all whose leaves are withered," they reasoned that American writers would, in time, produce works of novelty and freshness. In the past, American writers had imitated English authors and done that badly. Only when Americans declared their independence, ceasing to import English styles as merchants did English manufacturers, would American authorship come of age.[12]

Despite this greater responsiveness to the beauty of the physical world and to the subjective emotions aroused by nature, Buckminster insisted upon the importance of education in the classics. As alarmed by "the foul spirit of innovation" as Gardiner or Kirkland, Buckminster, in his justly famous lecture on "The Dangers and Duties of Men of Letters," urged scholars to drink at the wells of antiquity, to embrace the discipline required to master tradition, and to honor the "rules of taste" that had been established over time.[13] Also like the conservatives, Buckminster insisted that critics had a responsibility to judge the work of authors from the Olympian heights erected upon these traditions—"to expose absurdities, to check the contagion of false taste, to rescue the public from the impositions of dullness, and to assert the majesty of learning and truth."[14]

The fears of the conservatives and probably of Buckminster were summed up by Theodore Dehon. "It is with literature, as with government," he wrote. "Neither is a subject of perpetual experiment. The principles of both are fixed. They spring from sources and have relations, which are unchangeable and eternal." If writers disregard the models and rules laid down by tradition and instead delight "on the bosom of a cloud," it is not surprising, Dehon concluded, that "the world of letters should be overrun with Centaurs."[15] When the members of the society dined together on champagne, widgeons, and teal, the centaurs feared by Dehon sat among them. Though certainly not romanticists in the full sense of the word, Dana, Walter, and their ally Benjamin Welles did bring to the *Anthology* anticipations of the newer literary movements in England.

The Centaurs Invade the
Monthly Anthology Society

These "centaurs" had a love for the physical world and a feeling for its spiritual significance that set them apart from the conservatives. For them the beauty and variety of nature, its vastness and mystery, were more compelling evidence of God's existence than all of Newton's formulas. "Nature is beauty," Edmund Dana wrote, "and her most peculiar feature, variety."[16] While the Augustans loved the serenity and order of formal gardens, Edmund Dana and his friends thrilled to the feelings aroused by woodlands, marshes, and seashore. Benjamin Welles, who wrote the most impassioned account of the spiritual significance of nature, described the solitary lover of nature as one who, without fear of the excesses forbidden by reason, surrenders to "every great passion" and "riots in indulgence, more rapturous by progression, and more vacant by excess."[17] Every individual, Welles claimed, has a capacity for experience that is usually crushed by social conventions. If men but understood that the love of nature is spiritual, attesting to "an intimate connection and grand alliance" between man and God, they would, he insisted, trust their own noble natures more and the conventions of society less.[18]

For the radicals, literary genius was the human expression of the untamed forces of nature. Arthur Maynard Walter defined genius as "a divine spirit, a kind of fury, a madness, and enthusiasm—bursting through the confinement of reason."[19] While conservatives thought that great poetry and art could be created only by following universally valid rules, the radicals envisioned the development of new artistic forms, expressive of original responses to experience. They called for a recognition of the visionary truths of genius and for a more generous and sympathetic literary criticism. They felt that only if writers were free to construct their imagined worlds in their own way could they approach in art the variousness of nature. An Augustan suspicion of originality, Edmund Dana argued, was responsible for the inferiority of American literary efforts. The pursuit of imperfections has addled the brains of our critics, he complained. They weigh the beauties of poetry with all the sensitivity of "mechanicks [measuring] the dimensions of timber." We have become "hagridden by the classics," and "surfeited by repetitions of repetitions."[20] In this age of "hypercriticism" he concluded, "we have striven to be faultless, and neglected to be natural."[21]

The ideas expressed by Dana, Walter, and Welles were a blend of
the traditional and the iconoclastic. Although they loved a rough, un-
tended nature and literature and art that conveyed a passionate and
personal view of life, they remained trapped within the assumptions
of eighteenth-entury commonsense realism. They were bound, as were
the conservative members of the Monthly Anthology Society, to the
belief that the external world reported by the senses is truer than the
fictional worlds created by the imagination. Edmund Dana wrote that
"the superiority of nature over art, is the superiority of the works of
heaven over those of man."[22] Welles insisted that the pleasure of experiencing nature was more valid than any imaginative meditation on
the experience, because the first was a response to sensible truths
while the latter was at one remove, second-hand, and somehow
illusory.

The only grounds offered by the radicals for claiming the validity
of private, subjective experience lay in the analogy they drew between
the variousness of nature and the individuality of the mind. Commonsense realism, which identified truth with the reliability of the
mind's perception of the eternal world, stood in the way of a positive
belief in the artist's subjective experience. In spite of their trust that
the love of nature testified to a spiritual connection between God and
humanity, their faith in commonsense realism offered no way of demonstrating this connection. The breakthrough that ushered in romanticism, anticipated to some extent by Edmund Burke and Joseph
Buckminster, came only when justifications were found for claiming
that truth and beauty do not exist objectively but are the results of
the poet's imaginative reconstruction of his or her experience.

The assault on the Augustan literary values carried out by the radicals was largely negative. They identified the assumptions against
which the thrust of romantic ideas might be directed, but they failed
to fashion an aesthetics capable of translating the love of nature and
variety into art forms that affirmed an intuitive vision of the world.
This was the task taken up by Richard Henry Dana.

At the time, Dana was no more than an interested spectator, yet
the tension between the Augustans and the radicals at the Anthology
Society profoundly influenced his future. He not only was attracted
to the life of the writer, but also saw that literature was more deeply
concerned with the issues that mattered to people than philosophy or
quite possibly the law was. His brother Edmund helped persuade him
that expulsion from Harvard was a mark of glory, not a stigma, and

Edmund identified the poets and aestheticians who offered the most interesting alternatives to the curriculum at Harvard. More important, Edmund and his friends did the groundwork essential to Richard Henry Dana's breakthrough into romanticism. Although ten years passed before he was in a position to help found a successor to the *Monthly Anthology,* he never lost interest in the issues first raised in its pages.

Law and Politics

With Edmund's example before him and his own interests and talents in mind, Richard Henry Dana would probably have chosen to become a writer. Such hopes seemed crushed, however, when his oldest brother Francis speculated away the family fortune in 1804. Hoping to capitalize on the economic boom brought about by the Napoleonic Wars, Francis had mortgaged the family's landholdings to invest large sums in the construction of docks and wharves on land bordering the Charles River. No mercantile activity developed and the venture failed. To cover his son's debts, Judge Dana was forced into the humiliating expedient of selling the family mansion. Francis fled to Russia on the pretext of recouping his losses. This failure was a real blow to Richard Dana for it deprived him of an independent source of income without which no writer in America could expect to survive at that time. Many years later, he continued to look back on these events with bitterness. In a letter to William A. Jones, a New York writer whose outward circumstances were remarkably like his own, he wrote: "To be born in low life & poor, & to have to struggle all one's days against poverty, is hard enough; but I believe we may both feel what must be the difference between such a consideration, & that of having been born in the upper ranks & with a fair fortune, & then, to be cast down."[23]

The family's financial disaster placed enormous pressure on Dana to pursue a career in the law. Because neither of his older brothers was willing to enter the traditional family profession—Francis had disappeared in Russia and Edmund wrote for the *Monthly Anthology* while apparently living off a small allowance—the burden fell upon him. He faced the prospect with a heavy heart. Noting his reluctance and depression, his grandfather Ellery urged him on to active and socially useful work. "An indolent dronish life, is not the proper life of a man," he warned. "You did not seem when I talked with you on this

subject to incline to be a merchant, a physician or divine—you must
be something, and all things considered, I would advise you hereafter
to study the law."[24] His father's imminence loomed before him, however, and Dana felt incapable of living up to such an awesome model.
Convinced that he lacked the qualities necessary for worldly success,
angry that his brightest hopes had been snatched from him, he was
overcome by feelings of dread and helplessness. The death of his
mother in August 1807 added to his misery. Paralyzed by grief and
dispirited by the meaninglessness of life, he confessed to his sister
Martha that if, "by the stretching forth of my hand [I] could obtain
. . . riches and honours I could not summon the resolution to raise
it from my side."[25]

For a time, the family's financial situation was so desperate that
Judge Dana could not afford to pay the costs of sending his son to
study law in an office in Boston. Reprieved, Dana again sought refuge
with his grandfather in Newport. While there he read philosophy,
English literature, and criticism and prepared in a vague, undisciplined way for his future. When Martha wrote expressing concern
over her brother's apparent lack of ambition, Ellery replied: "He may
be said to be diffident, but it is an ambition to excell, and an apprehension that he shall not arrive at preeminence which seems to discourage him."[26]

In 1809 Dana finally began his apprenticeship in the law offices of
his cousin Francis Dana Channing. Although initially challenged by
the task of making sense out of Sir Edward Coke's "mighty chaos of
learning" and by the prospect of earning his own way, Dana soon
grew discouraged when President Madison's policy of restricting trade
with Britain and France led to an economic depression. His cousin
and fellow apprentice Edward Tyrell Channing described the situation: young lawyers without employment were to be seen lounging
on the "sunny side of Cornhill [Street], . . . with their hands behind
them" and their pockets empty, "groaning about the times" and discussing neither law nor politics but literature.[27] Pessimistic in the
best of times, Dana was now unnerved by the very real prospect of
failure. In fulfilling his responsibilities to the family, he had followed
a career for which he felt unsuited. Now he feared that he would be
pointed out on the streets of Boston as Judge Dana's third unsuccessful son.

After Francis Channing left for Europe in 1810, Judge Dana took
over responsibility for his son's legal training. At about this same

time, Dana fell in love with Ruth Charlotte Smith, a schoolteacher from Providence, Rhode Island. According to family tradition, Judge Dana opposed this match on the grounds that his son ought not to marry so far beneath his station. Dana's resentment may be inferred from remarks, made later in a short story, deploring marriages contracted for reasons of status: they might as well be made by proxy, he commented.

Within a year of his father's death in 1811, Dana set out for Baltimore to complete his studies in the office of Robert Goodloe Harper. He hoped that the economic situation would be better and lawyers fewer in Baltimore than in Boston. On his way through New York, he bought a set of lottery tickets. Because he was not a gambling man and could hardly remember a time when his luck had been anything but bad, he must have bought them as a fatalistic gesture motivated by a perverse desire to prove to himself the utter futility of his position. His luck held—the tickets were worthless.

On his way south, he wrote a letter to his sister expressing his fear of failure and his desire to end the last obstacles to his marriage:

To one who has felt from the earliest moments of reflection that he could be happy only in domestick life, whose visions of future enjoyment set before his mind the quiet & deep felt scene of his home & fireside, to such a one, my sister, it is indeed a hard condition to be torn from a home which every day is made more dear, from a being too who is intertwined with every better feeling of the heart. . . . I wish I could rid myself of the continual dread I feel lest I should at last be compelled to return with all my endeavors counteracted, & hopes blasted. Should it be so, my only wish is that death may soon put an end to all. I cannot bear to think that I shall ever live to be pointed at. And what, too, would there be for me to live for?[28]

Although melancholy and a preoccupation with death were fashionable among Dana and his friends, his despair was more than a literary pose. No longer able to claim a place among New England's moneyed elite and doubtful of his ability to make his own way among the new, ambitious professional classes, Dana longed to escape the frustrations and disappointments of life. His brief service in Harper's law office did nothing to enhance his opinion of the profession. Already convinced that most lawyers were "quacks" and "blockheads," he saw little reason to change his mind after his encounter with the blustering, egotistical Harper.

After his admission to the Baltimore County Bar in 1812, Dana tried to establish an office in western New York only to discover that his certification did not qualify him to practice in that state. At the age of twenty-five, he finally began his law practice in the small rural town of Sutton, Massachusetts, equally distant between Cambridge and Ruth Charlotte Smith's home in Providence. Although Sutton lay in a lovely setting of ponds surrounded by well-tended fields and in full view of Mount Wachusetts, life there soon disabused him of the charms of a pastoral existence.

Bored by inactivity and the dull routine of daily life, and irritated by the narrowness and conceit of the people, Dana appreciated as never before the truth of Cowper's depressing portrait of life in rural England. In a letter to Edward Channing, he confessed: "I have lost all powers of feeling or of thought or rather am sensible only to an uneasiness as if some undefined, shapeless evil was coming on me. . . . I never shall have command of my intellect again till I am happy."[29]

Early in the spring of 1813, Dana moved his practice to Cambridgeport, just outside Boston, and in May of the same year he married Ruth Charlotte. With five hundred dollars borrowed from his brother and sisters, he bought furnishings for the house he had rented, reporting to his grandfather that he was at last a happy man. A year later his first child, Ruth Charlotte, was born. He and his wife had three more children, Richard Henry Dana, Jr., born in 1815, Edmund ("Ned") born in 1818, and a second daughter, Susan, born in 1820.

Soon after Dana's move to Cambridgeport, he was drawn into the efforts of the Federalist party to wrest political power from the Jeffersonian Republicans. In 1814 he was invited by the Washington Benevolent Society of Cambridge to deliver the Fourth of July oration. Because he was anxious to distinguish himself and believed that the occasion might increase his legal business, he accepted the invitation. His speech was highly partisan, even exceeding the bitterness and invective that might have been expected at such an event. The oration was an act of filial loyalty, a son's acknowledgement of the rage and sense of betrayal that his father, the irascible judge, felt at the course taken by the Republicans. At a deeper level, however, the speech testified to his own sense of displacement. It was a protest against the utopian faith of the nation regarding progress and reason. It was the response of a man who, foreseeing no place for himself in the new order of things, exalted the qualities of heart and mind that would dignify his revolt.

The political philosophy that Dana defended in his oration was derived more from the ideas of Edmund Burke than from the beliefs of the architects of the Constitution. Edmund Burke's ideas appealed to Dana for the same reasons that the poetry of William Cowper, James Thomson, and Thomas Gray did: they all revered the past, appreciated the organic nature of social institutions, and loved the individuality and eccentricity encouraged by social distinctions and traditional practices. Ignoring the fact that the Federalists had, like the Jeffersonians, sipped the heady wine of eighteenth-century rationalism, Dana cast the mantle of Burke around the old Federalists. He claimed that they had been guided less by abstract reasoning than by an understanding of human nature. In their hands, religion, family, property, and traditions had been secured and the integrity of community life preserved. Recognizing that people's fears and prejudices rest upon experience, the Federalists had fashioned a constitution that, Dana said, depended "not on the virtues alone, but on the exact balance of our very vices."[30]

Like Burke, Dana distrusted the abstract, a priori political theories of Enlightenment thinkers. He rejected the principles of equality, human perfectibility, and "absolute liberty" as notions "formed to flatter the vanity, confirm the pride, and excite and indulge the licentious passions of our nature."[31] His harshest invectives were reserved for Jefferson, a man who, Dana declaimed, "has cared and thought more about the mammoth, than about a fellow-being; for the very philosophical reason that he is a great deal the bigger of the two."[32] Only a "philosopher" and a "theorist" could believe that the human community was bound together by nothing more than popular consent. According to Dana, Jefferson and his followers, blinded by "their own mad systems" had looked upon the sinews that bind a community "with the curious, unmoved intentness of the chemist in an analyzing process."[33] In their quest for perfection, he insisted, they had come dangerously close to destroying the traditions and institutions that make social life possible.

Dana associated the optimistic, utopian dreams that sprang up at the time of the Revolution with this same strain of abstract, rationalist thought. He opened his speech with a blunt assault on the Republicans' version of the Adamic myth:

The day which we have met to celebrate, we once vainly imagined, was to work an universal change in the condition and character of man; that it was to spread its light over the nations which we supposed were sitting in the

gloom of slavery, ignorance and crime; and that they were to come forth the
renovated beings of freedom, wisdom and virtue. . . . The world, with its
swamps and deserts, was shooting forth in all the beauty and freshness of
Eden; and man walking in the midst, sinless and free as Adam. But, alas!
all that our fevered imaginations pictured out was but a dream. . . . Human
nature has not yet reached the stage of perfectibility in which laws are but
useless entanglements, and the power of government but a cumbrous restraint upon virtue.[34]

From the time of John Winthrop, the first governor of the Massachusetts Bay Colony, Americans believed that they were to occupy a
special place in human history. Beginning fresh in a new land, they
would prepare the way for the redemption or enlightenment of mankind. Although this myth had inspired conservatives and liberals
alike, John Adams as well as Thomas Jefferson, Dana was convinced
that it was nothing more than a grand but foolish, perhaps even dangerous, delusion.

His rejection of this myth, his tendency to associate optimistic nationalism with such delusions, was to have an enduring influence on
his development as a writer. By denying the validity of this idea, he
placed himself at a psychic distance from the native themes and materials that inspired many of America's most successful writers. The
cause of literary nationalism would never move Dana as it did many
of his contemporaries. He was too close to the shattering events of
the French Revolution, his personal history was too entwined in the
disappointments and suspicions of the old Federalists for him to sym-
pathize with the literary possibilities of the American experience.

Although his oration revealed his willingness to join in efforts to
revitalize the Federalist cause, Dana could not sustain for long an enthusiasm for the ambitions of the young, tough-minded Federalists of
his own generation. He would never feel at home among this new
Brahmin class that rose out of the failures of the old Federalists. Their
dream of creating an American Augustan Age based on an alliance of
true scholars and newly rich merchants and manufacturers struck him
as self-serving and crass. He distrusted their faith in progress, their
blatant desire for money, property, and status, and their pretentious
claim to authority in matters of taste. He had no stomach for court-
room combat and little talent for the easygoing ways necessary in an
age when the practice of law was inseparable from the practice of politics. Edward T. Channing jokingly advised Dana that if he wished to
succeed in the law he must "go to the tavern & smoke, drink flip,

and talk with the citizens—Speak in all Town-meetings, and be a man of consequence."[35] For the shy and reserved Dana, the camaraderie expected of the attorney was infinitely more repellent than the obscurities of Sir Edward Coke.

He was at home neither in the reactionary world of his father nor in the new order being created by tougher, younger Federalists. Although he shared his father's reverence for tradition and the system of deference that placed leadership in the hands of the wealthy and learned, he sensed that he would come to grief if he tried to live by his father's expectations. Intellectually as well as temperamentally, Dana could not accept many of the ideas and values that shored up the eighteenth-century world of his father. At the same time, he scorned the selfishness and materialism of the new professional and commercial classes. He was increasingly convinced that he was too sensitive and possessed talents too refined for success in the new order. His brother Edmund offered an alternative: his preromatic ideas and slightly raffish aura made the role of the rebel vaguely attractive. This course too held perils because it invited the indolent and dronish life his grandfather had warned against. Richard Henry Dana was literally trapped. Disgusted by his education at Harvard and forced by circumstances to pursue a career he loathed, he was receptive to ideas that seemed to promise a new way of understanding and experiencing the world.

Chapter Two
Romantic Critic for the *North American Review*

When Dana's disgust with the practice of law became more than he could bear, he turned to literature as a sanctuary from adversity and failure. Although he pursued his legal career in a halfhearted fashion until 1819, he had few clients. With time on his hands, he indulged in his passion for English literature and criticism. He was drawn to the brooding, introspective poetry of William Collins and Thomas Gray. In the lyric poetry of William Cowper, he discovered a piety, delicacy of feeling, and contempt for worldly affairs that answered his own mood. His reading strengthened his conviction that the Enlightenment preoccupation with the surface of experience, its relentless quest for order and intelligibility, drained life of its joy and mystery, nature of its moral suggestiveness, and people of their capacity for originality.

By 1817 when Dana joined with friends in publishing the *North American Review,* he had resolved the dilemma that ensnared his brother Edmund and fellow radicals of the Monthly Anthology Society. In their effort to escape the Augustan reverence for the universal in human experience, they had elevated nature, in all its variousness, above art; however, Dana discovered grounds for trusting the artist's subjective experiences in the works of Archibald Alison, William Wordsworth, and Samuel Coleridge. In the reviews that Dana wrote for the *North American Review* between 1817 and 1819, he consistently advocated romantic ideas and critical standards. There were, among Dana's contemporaries, critics who championed the poetry of Byron and Wordsworth. There were also writers who praised the superficial romantic enthusiasm for ancient mythology and legends and exotic places and customs. But Dana, alone among critics writing in the period before the American Renaissance, steadfastly evaluated works of literature in terms of a theory of the imagination that stressed the mind's creative powers and its collaborative relationship with nature.

The Education of a Romanticist

It is impossible to reconstruct with certainty the intellectual process through which Dana found an alternative to what was for him
the dead end of neoclassicism. Acting on the conviction that diaries
are inevitably dishonest, he "committed to the flames every scrap of
the records of [his] feelings and thoughts."[1] He asked his grandfather
to burn the letters he had written during the crucial years from 1808
to 1815. It seems clear, however, from internal evidence, that his in-
duction into a romantic aesthetics began sometime during this period
with his reading of the English aesthetician Archibald Alison's *Essays
in the Nature and Principles of Taste.*[2] Alison, whose ideas about the
imagination were more far-reaching than Burke's, introduced a subjectivity into aesthetic theory that was vital to the development of
Dana's romanticism.

The earlier aestheticians—Joshua Reynolds, Joseph Addison, and
Thomas Reid—had claimed that the quality of beauty is an attribute
existing objectively in the things observed. They also believed that
the mind possesses a special faculty, analogous to the five senses, for
perceiving this quality. It followed from this "aesthetic objectivism"
that judgments of taste were statements of fact based upon a mirror-
like correspondence between the nature of external things and the
structure of the human mind.

Alison overturned these ideas by arguing persuasively that the
quality of beauty is not the object of immediate observation but is
ascribed to forms and sounds by the imagination. The perception of
a beautiful object, he explained, arouses in the mind of the beholder
a series of associations linking that object to images, sounds, memories, and ideas that seem to possess similar qualities of expression.
The poet and artist strive not to describe what they have observed but
to express their ideas and associations in such a way that others may
share in the unique inwardness of the experience. Alison assumed that
the process of association operates in a roughly uniform way among
all members of a society. Nevertheless, his recognition of the subjective sources of the imagination was just the dynamite required to
blow up the aesthetic certainties of neoclassical critics.[3] His ideas discouraged mimicry of classical models, for he insisted that by canoniz-
ing traditional tastes, critics were ignoring the wonderful variety of
human experience. Alison also warned against what Edmund Dana
had called "hypercriticism." He pointed out that an overriding con-

cern with arriving at critical judgments was destroying sensitivity to beauty.[4]

Alison provided Dana not only with a more subjective aesthetics but also with a deeper understanding of the possible connections between beauty and moral truth. Before Alison, aestheticians had argued that moral truths, like the quality of beauty, exist objectively in the natural order of things. These moral truths were thought to have a sensory quality, possibly even a visual one, perceptible to the moral sense. The mechanistic way in which this connection between nature and moral truth was viewed is reflected in the conventions that governed the use of imagery. Poets employed the imagery of the ocean to suggest God's infinitude and the majesty of the mountains to evoke the grandeur of creation. Joseph Addison, for example, argued that nature instructs her admirer in moral truths literally by enlarging the capacity of the mind to encompass the immensity of God. Alison, on the other hand, believed that moral truths do not exist objectively in nature any more than the qualities of beauty do. They too are ascribed as signs or expressions of the moral constitution of humanity: "Whenever [the objects of the material world] afford us delight, they are always the signs or expressions of higher qualities, by which our moral sensibilities are called forth. . . . There is not one of these features of scenery which is not fitted to awaken us to moral emotions; to lead us, when once the key of our imagination is struck, to trains of fascinating and endless imagery, and with indulgence of them, to make our bosoms glow with conceptions of mental excellence, or melt in the dreams of moral good."[5] Alison opened up the rich symbolic possibilities of imagery drawn from nature. Because the process by which moral significance is ascribed to nature must, to some degree, depend on the experiences of each individual and because everything in nature can awaken the moral emotions, the potential of natural imagery is endless.

Wordsworth's poetry, which Dana read for the first time during the year or so before becoming associated with the *North American Review,* embodied many of the ideas that he had first encountered in Alison's *Essays.* At a time when, to most Americans, Wordsworth "served for little else than a travesty to the wittling, smartness to the reviewer, and for a sneer to the fastidious pretender to taste," Dana declared that he was the most important and original poet of the age.[6] He admired Wordsworth most for his ability to alter the way the reader experiences nature. The immediacy of Wordsworth's poetry, he thought, was not the result of mere accurate descriptions of the physical world but of a "change wrought in ourselves." In reading Wordsworth, he wrote, we experience nature for the first time in all its suggestive moral richness:

A moral sense is given to all things; and the materials of the earth which seemed made only for homely uses, become the teachers of our minds and ministers of good to our hearts. Here the love of beauty is made religion, and what we had falsely esteemed the indulgence of idle imaginations, is found to have higher and more serious purposes, than the staid affairs of life. The world of nature is full of magnificence and beauty; every thing in it is made to more than a single end. . . . In the luxury of this higher existence, we find a moral strength, and from the riot of imagination comes our holiest calm.[7]

Dana believed that Wordsworth was the first poet to make the spiritual connection between an individual and nature the essential principle of his poetry. We read him, Dana said, and the blinders fall from our eyes. No longer the prisoners of our five senses, we are able to bring to any experience of nature our own associations and thus participate with the poet in the imaginative contemplation of nature. Alison and Wordsworth helped him realize that the imagination enables the poet to arrive at truths above logic and fact. They validated his hunger for a more spiritual and subjective understanding of man's relationship to the world.

Coleridge, however, touched Dana at a far deeper level. Dana's sympathy with Coleridge went beyond shared ideas to include what the philosopher William James once described as the "more or less dumb sense of what life honestly and deeply means, . . . [the] individual way of just seeing and feeling the total push and press of the cosmos."[8] Encountering Coleridge's work for the first time must have stunned Dana with the proverbial shock of recognition, for in Coleridge he discovered a writer whose mind and temperament answered to his own.

Dana probably learned about Coleridge's work as early as 1809. His brother Edmund's friend Washington Allston met Coleridge in Rome in 1805. The two men spent many hours together at Allston's home at Olevanna Romana, outside Rome, discussing art, aesthetics, and psychology. When Allston returned to the United States for a brief visit in 1809, he discussed Coleridge's ideas with the two Dana

brothers. Because Allston was in London in 1817, the year that Coleridge's *Biographia Literaria* was published, it is quite possible that he
forwarded the book to the Danas. In a review article written for the
North American Review in 1819, Richard Dana alluded to ideas in the
Biographia, revealing a familiarity with its contents to be found in no
other literary criticism of the period. Not until the publication of
Aids to Reflection in 1825 was Coleridge's work read with sympathy;
not until the 1840s did his contribution to philosophical aesthetics
have a significant impact on literary criticism in America.

Dana's affinity with Coleridge had roots that he could not have
fully appreciated at the time. The similarities in their temperaments
sprang from their experiences of social displacement. Estranged from
their social castes, forced by the uncertainties of the literary life to
lead the insecure, classless careers of professional authors, they both
had difficulty adapting to what they regarded as the philistinism and
ugliness of the contemporary world. They bore the cost of their alienation in depression, melancholy, and illness. Coleridge's motives for
writing the *Biographia* struck a responsive chord in Dana. Anxious to
arouse the intellectuals of his day to the dangers inherent in egalitarianism, materialism, and intellectual skepticism, Coleridge addressed the very fears that Dana had inherited from his Federalist
background. He was for Dana the exemplar of genius, a lonely visionary driven to decipher the secrets of the universe regardless of the
risks to his reputation and public esteem.

A decade before American readers recognized anything more than
an impenetrable mysticism in the *Biographia Literaria,* Dana began to
assimilate the metaphysical and aesthetic ideas presented in the book.
In Coleridge's attack on the psychological theories of John Locke and
the mechanistic association theory of David Hartley, Dana found support for his own conviction that the writers of the eighteenth century
had ignored the "delightful mystery within us."[9] Coleridge portrayed
the life of an author in heroic terms, casting the poet in the role of a
godlike being whose imagination is governed by creative powers similar to those that operate in the divine mind. It was a notion that
initially appealed to Dana but one that would haunt and trouble him
as well. The *Biographia Literaria* also addressed Dana's concern about
the inadequacy of neoclassical standards of literary criticism. Coleridge's assessment of the school of Johnson and Pope and his lengthy
evaluation of Wordsworth's *Literary Ballads* embodied new critical
standards that Dana sought to make his own.

Dana learned most from Coleridge's insight into the dynamic processes of the imagination. In the *Biographia,* Coleridge explained how the poet changes the material forms of the world into the spiritual truths of the imagination, dissolving experience in order to create a more personal, beautiful, and psychologically truthful vision of the world. Coleridge's explanation of how the imagination transforms all things to the poet's mood struck Dana as convincing evidence of the predominance of the mind over sensory experience and the superiority of the imagination over discursive reasoning. The influence of Coleridge can be seen, for example, in one of Dana's many attempts to state the essential character of the imagination. "The poetical mind," Dana wrote, "may be said to see, and not to see; all is absorbed deeply inward, and goes in mingling with emotions, and fancies of the brain, changing its shapes and relations in its very course."[10]

For all his sympathy with Coleridge's ideas, Dana lacked, in these early years, the philosophical sophistication to grasp his difficult and demanding arguments. He could appreciate neither the importance that Coleridge attached to the principle of organic unity in poetry nor his explanation of the dialectical nature of the imagination. Because he looked upon literature as a refuge from the materialism and mediocrity of his day, Dana was sometimes more conscious of Coleridge's theory of the imagination as an escape from the tyranny of prudential concerns than as the foundation of a new, transcendental metaphysics. If Dana could not comprehend all the implications of Coleridge's views, he understood enough to free himself from the literary loyalties of his generation.

The Founding of the *North American Review*

Since his undergraduate days at Harvard, Dana had been torn between the practice of law, urged upon him by his father and grandfather, and the life of a writer, represented for him by his eccentric brother Edmund. By 1815 his emancipation from this struggle was nearly over. His dissatisfaction with the practice of law cleared away his last hesitations. Carried beyond the confusions of the Anthology Society radicals by his reading of Alison, Wordsworth, and Coleridge, he was at last ready to take up the cause of literary romanticism. But there was no periodical in America that would have welcomed his literary opinions. The old *Monthly Anthology* had ceased publication in 1811, a victim of the members' busy professional schedules, the casual editorial policy, and the quarrels over literary and religious issues.[11] The *Portfolio,* published in Philadelphia and edited by Charles Coldwell (1814–16), had a reputation, not wholly deserved, for eclecticism and a devotion to the principles of Pope and Johnson. What the country needed was a new literary journal.

In the winter of 1814–15, Dana joined his cousin Edward T. Channing, John Kirkland, and Willard Phillips in drawing up a prospectus for the new venture. A letter that Channing wrote in 1815 suggests the enthusiasm and, incidentally, the Brahmin bias of the group: "How you would have laughed, could you have peeped into my snug office, for two or three days past, & seen the great men, learned Doctors of Law & of Divinity, Tutors at College, Editors & publishers, holding solemn debate on the Magazine;—one writing a prospectus, another talking about style, a third (more wise than all) counting the cost & the chances of success."[12]

When William Ellery learned of his grandson's involvement in the scheme, he grew genuinely alarmed. He warned Dana: "If poetry & sentiment would afford a decent subsistence to those who abound in them, I should have nothing to say against poets and sentimentalists; but man is an eating animal, and, as [Erasmus] Darwin says, he must eat or be eaten, and it is also said that a great majority of those who have devoted their time to the pleasures of imagination have lived dependent and died beggars."[13] Ellery's was a fair assessment of the prospects facing the aspiring writer in America in the first decades of the nineteenth century. No writer had yet succeeded in making a livelihood from his literary efforts. Institutional supports for literature hardly existed. Periodicals were too few in number and too poor to pay contributors adequate fees. A preference for the work of British writers also made it difficult for an American author to find an audience. Although in 1815 he probably still thought of literature as an avocation, Dana was not, in any case, willing to let the fear of failure put him off any longer.

The plans of Dana and his friends had to be laid aside, however, when William Tudor, a member of the old Anthology Society, returned from Europe and "desired that, as he had come home to publish a periodical of like character, his work might take the place of [their] projected one, & there ended [the] literary project."[14] Tudor took on the periodical almost single-handed. He not only was the sole proprietor and editor of the first four volumes of the *North American Review and Miscellaneous Journal* but also wrote three-fourths of the articles. When he retired from the editorship in March 1817, he transferred the ownership of the journal to Willard Phillips. Jared Sparks was named the editor and an association of contributors was formed, which included Richard Henry Dana, Edward Tyrell Channing, Nathan Hale, John Gallison, and William Powell Mason.[15] In March 1818, Channing became the editor and named Dana as his editorial assistant.

Dana felt as if his years of disappointment and frustration were over. For his part in managing the journal, he received the princely fee of five hundred dollars, a sum that seemed to promise financial independence in a career that he had dreamed of since his undergraduate days. He had never been so busy or so happy. In addition to finding contributors and overseeing publication, Dana wrote five articles for the *Review*. His letters to his grandfather, which had formerly been suffused with a gloomy stoicism, took on a sprightliness and almost boyish eagerness. He reported that his health, which had been poor for years, was improving. Ellery reconciled himself to his grandson's literary career only because Dana was being paid for it. Because he had been a revolutionary in his own right, Ellery was probably more amused than irritated when Dana declared his and Channing's intentions of attacking the older man's *"Popeish* notions of poetry, & Dean Swift prose."[16]

Literary Nationalism

During these early years, contributors to the *North American Review* were preoccupied with the issue of literary nationalism. In general, Americans' national pride had been heightened by the few successes in the War of 1812 and vexed by the disparaging comments of British literary critics and travelers. Those concerned with culture were particularly anxious to prove that America could produce writers to equal those of Britain. Archibald Alison gave focus to this issue because his theory of association implied that nationalistic writing is best.[17] He had suggested that associations based on the landscape, history, traditions, and customs shared by the people of a nation are the ones most likely to arouse the emotions of beauty and sublimity. Writers for the *Review* debated whether America offered material of sufficient distinctiveness and abundance to provide the basis of a national literature.

Dana's cousin Walter Channing initiated the discussion in 1815 when he published a dismayingly pessimistic piece, asserting that America had no national character. Without either a different language or a unique racial identity and with a long relationship of colonial dependency, Americans could not, in Walter Channing's opinion, produce a literature of their own. In an influential essay written in 1816, his brother Edward Tyrell Channing expressed the hope that if Americans could not create a literature significantly different from the British, they could at least produce an independent one. The literature of a country, he wrote, should be just "as domestick and individual, as its character or political institutions. Its charm is its nativeness." Edward urged American writers to take pride in "the fantastick superstitions of your fathers," and the "lonely fairy scenes, that lie far back in the mists of your fables."[18] And so the issue was joined. Contributors rushed forward with a variety of suggestions about the native materials offered by the American experience. William Tudor recommended the use of Indian fables, John Gorham Palfrey saw possibilities in Puritan heroism, William Cullen Bryant felt that the diversity of American regional and ethnic types offered resources as rich as any Walter Scott had found in the legends and peoples of the Scottish highlands.[19]

Dana sided neither with the confident proponents of a national literature nor with the skeptics. Although committed to recognizing native talent when it appeared, he was not a literary nationalist. He believed that great literature is created by individuals of genius: imagination knows no nationality. He acknowledged that English critics were too often harsh and unfair, but they also spoke the truth: "An American library, would, we fancy, be rather a sorry and heartsickening spectacle to a literary man." There would be time enough, he added, to discard English literary traditions when American writers "shall be so broad and liberal, that the authors of England shall become dangerous to our freedom of mind, and . . . corrupting and degrading [to] our natures."[20] Dana loved the old English poets too much and owed too great a debt to the ideas of Coleridge to play the role of an ingrate. Moreover, he distrusted the romanticism, whether English, Scottish, or German, that stressed the genius of national character. The associations that played upon national characteristics were, from his point of view, little better than Augustan cravings for the universal. Neither did justice to the unique visions of the solitary seeker.

The inferiority of American culture, he believed, was due neither

to a dependence on British writers nor to the absence of shared associations, but rather to the national character itself. The obsession with
material progress, the leveling effects of democracy, and the absence
of a wealthy class committed to promoting the arts created an atmosphere in which serious culture could not thrive. Americans did not
honor their writers and artists. "This universal talent for action," he
complained, prejudices the popular mind against the man of letters.
Poets are dismissed as "intellectual idlers," and those who are moved
by any motive but the thought of gain are considered unmanly. If a
work of literature comes out, he commented, "it is made a cause of
lament that so much talent should be thus thrown away."[21]

Contributors to the *Review* expressed concern about the influence of
democracy on culture. Economic changes and egalitarianism were, in
their view, undermining the authority of the "better sort" over matters of taste. To meet this challenge, they discussed forming an alliance with the new entrepreneurial class. They hoped to educate and
uplift the tastes of these new men. Like their conservative predeces-
sors of the old Monthly Anthology Society, they also proposed to im-
prove the quality of education in the colleges of the nation, to
encourage a reverence for the classics, and to create new cultural institutions that would support their Brahmin order.

Because Dana had been cut adrift from his social moorings by the
dramatic collapse of the family's fortunes, his thoughts about the
questions of class and culture were ambiguous. He shared his friends'
concern about the influence of democracy, but not their enthusiasm
for an alliance with the business class. He did dream, in a nostalgic
way, about the creation of a patronage system that would allow writers to write as they pleased while living on the largess of wealthy
benefactors. In practice, however, he felt only contempt for the business class. An honorable writer, he argued, must stand in opposition
to the forces of progress that such businessmen command. He was
skeptical too of the plans to reform the cultural institutions of the
nation. Colleges like Harvard and Yale might encourage talent, he
conceded, but they were more likely than not to crush genius. "Men
of genius," he wrote, are "outlaws," envied and mistrusted by those
whose reputations are based on "acquisition, industry," and "studied
correctness alone."[22] A college course that stressed the classics and
conformity to rules and models was fatal to genius because it encouraged imitation and bred contempt for natural feelings and homely
beauties. "Original minds will be peculiar and individual," he con-

cluded, "and it is not for us to haggle at every thing new. . . . Those
who have produced what is lasting have always been fond of working
in their own way."[23]

Having rejected the alliance and the agenda proposed by his
friends, Dana had nowhere to turn but to the ordinary people. He
sometimes expressed confidence in their literary opinions. At least
they came to a work of literature without preconceptions: their responses were not dictated by outworn traditions or the prejudices of
some literary clique. He warned those concerned about the literary
character of the country against a "supercilious indifference to the
opinions of ordinary men"; yet he feared that once the majority were
in a position to dictate matters of taste, all originality, variety, and
eccentricity would be ruthlessly suppressed. He had no firm ground
on which to stand, therefore, and few allies anywhere. Because the
recognition of genius in 1818 was more threatening to the cultural
establishment than to the ordinary people, he was willing to defend
the propriety of the people's role in determining matters of taste.

Dana's Literary Reviews

Although Dana aspired to be a writer of poetry and fiction, his talents were probably best suited to the work of literary criticism. In
addition to his natural ability—an intelligent, critical mind and a
clear, vigorous writing style—he had the good (and bad) fortune to be
born in the nick of time. The circumstances of his life placed him at
the American watershed between two epochs in Western literary history. What is more important, he knew it. His reviews are therefore
distinguished by an unusual sensitivity to the important philosophical
and aesthetic issues separating neoclassicism from romanticism.
While his contemporaries were either defending Augustan values or
attempting to moderate romantic ones, he was boldly presenting the
subjective or idealistic way of experiencing the world and challenging
the claims of classicism and scientism. His reviews, whether of Irving's *Sketch Book* or of a book of poetry readings for children, were
illumined by a sure and steady sense of these larger issues.

In the struggle to win a sympathetic reading of this new romantic
literature, critics were beginning to practice a more relativistic and
historically grounded style of criticism. Dana embraced this new criticism. Having read the work of the European critics August and
Friedrich Schlegel and Madame de Staël, he insisted on the impor-

tance of understanding the historical forces—religion, law, and custom—that had shaped a writer's caste of thought. Against the Augustan critics who believed in the timelessness of literary standards, he urged readers to appreciate the special beauties of form and qualities of perception unique to each age and nationality. He helped offset the impression left by some neoclassical critics that the early English poets were superstitious and ignorant and that the Elizabethans were unacceptably uncouth. The critic, according to Dana, must understand the writer's intentions, clarify these for the reader, and judge the work by the writer's success in realizing his own design. A critic must have wide tastes, "be trammelled by no narrow systems or schools," and above all else, possess in his own right the imagination to be caught up in the author's act of creation.[24]

Dana developed a highly personal style of criticism. While other critics wrote encyclopedic essays composed in an impersonal voice, he expressed his likes, dislikes, and crotchets in a witty, outspoken, and direct way. He was too independent and courageous to flatter the vanities of American writers or cater to the prejudices of their readers. His reviews for the *North American Review* were fair, honest, and perceptive, enlivened by pungent, archaic Anglo-Saxon expressions and spirited attacks on the certitudes and pretensions of his day.

If Dana was the most outspoken supporter of romanticism among the contributors to the *North American Review*, he was not entirely without allies. At least he believed that Edward T. Channing and Willard Phillips comprised a little community of like-minded individuals. In later years, when Channing was the Boylston Professor of Rhetoric at Harvard, he earned a reputation for being a conservative and old-fashioned taskmaster; but in his salad days as editor for the *Review*, Channing gingerly opened the journal to the new currents of thought. Although he believed that aesthetic standards are unchanging, he admired genius and originality, urged a sympathetic style of criticism, and appreciated such early expressions of romanticism as Scott's novels and Byron's poetry.[25] Phillips was a "wide-liker" whose critical essays betrayed the inconsistencies of a dilettante. He admired the work of the morally conventional Maria Edgeworth and of the moral freebooter Lord Byron.[26] Phillips praised with equal enthusiasm the inferior, gaudy, Gothic novelist Charles Robert Maturin and James Fenimore Cooper. Phillip's criticism did nothing to clarify the literary principles of the *North American Review* but did provide some romantic writers a sympathetic reading.

At one time, Dana and Channing had thought they shared a true affinity, but they had, unknowingly perhaps, moved down different paths. Channing's literary education never went beyond that provided by the Scottish aestheticians and the poets of sensibility. He believed that the imagination and the emotions must be kept subordinate to reason. They were useful as the motivation for virtue and the source of beautiful associations when kept in check, but were dangerous when they undermined good sense. A bolder advocacy of romantic ideas would have seemed to Channing a threat to the class loyalties and career ambitions that tied him to the new social and economic order. Dana, on the other hand, had gone further because he was attracted by Coleridge's interest in the truths revealed by the imagination. If Dana's ideas posed no real threat to the new Brahmin order, they at least brought into question the easy fusion of optimism, reason, and sentimentality upon which it was based.

In each of his five essays, Dana pressed his case for romantic literature and aesthetic ideas. Like young critics before and since, he began his career as a reviewer by attacking the cultural assumptions of his day. His first essay, entitled "Old Times," presented a critique of the Enlightenment that had all the earmarks of the new romantic sensibility—a love of old things and remote times, a distrust of rationalism, a hatred of all kinds of conformity, and a conviction that the way to truth lay in a closer spiritual relationship to nature. The essay is essentially a lament for an age of naturalness and simplicity, which had been displaced by an age of artificial refinement and heartless rationality. The mood invoked by the essay is one of nostalgia. To the unwary reader, the author's obvious sympathy with a traditional system of deference might have suggested that the essay was the work of a disgruntled, elderly Federalist. The "old times" revered by Dana, however, is not a specific period in history, and certainly not the eighteenth century; instead, it is a mythical golden age—the age of bards and balladeers—when men of "self-trusting minds" acquired, through a closeness to rough and uncultivated nature, characters that combined "the natural and the tender, the imaginative and the manly."[27] Dana set this age when poetry thrived and individuality left its imprint on character and conduct against the Enlightenment, when "the utterance of strong feeling is ill-breeding and dissimulation, wisdom."[28]

His second essay, a review of Washington Allston's *Sylphs of the Seasons,* was largely a pretext for announcing the coming of a new era in poetry. In it, Dana declared the death of the old gods. According to Dana, Alexander Pope was a man of wit, strong sense, and sprightly fancy, but he was no poet. The popular William Cowper and Thomas Campbell were moralists whose imaginations had been sacrificed in "this lecture room of the Muses," and whose accomplishments were more suited to the age of Queen Anne than to the nineteenth century.[29] In the new poetry, Dana declared, there would be less drawing room artificiality, less finger-wagging morality, and less satire. People would be set free from the domesticated views of nature popular in the eighteenth century to experience nature as it truly is— wild and untamed, rich in associations, and suggestive of the kinship humans have to all things. As he said of this more democratic poetry: "It has thrown aside the distinctions of society, and treats of us all in common, as creatures of like passions. . . . With an enlarged philosophy, it teaches us that there is nothing vulgar but vice, and that there is scarce an object through the whole of existence, that is not in some way poetical to a truly poetical mind."[30] Dana commended Allston as a poet of the new school who possessed not only an "eye for nature" but also the imagination to penetrate to the "soul and sense" of things.[31]

He could have wished for a stronger representative of the new poetry. Allston was a better painter than poet. Allston's poems gave stronger evidence of his eye for color than of his imaginative or dramatic powers. In keeping with his belief in sympathetic criticism, Dana did what he could to suggest the artistic sensitivities that Allston brought to his poetry but was too honest a critic to overlook his faults. Although he was alive to beauty and a lover of nature, Allston was, according to Dana, afflicted with a "weak amiableness" that took the bite out of his social observations and the profundity and passion out of his poetry. Allston could not, as Byron did, take his readers into the dark and subterranean depths of the soul or, as Wordsworth did, make nature's solemn beauties illuminate humanity's spiritual longings. Such comparisons might be unfair, Dana admitted, but no concern for the literary reputation of the nation could disguise the fact that Allston's poetry was the work of an essentially simple and superficial nature.

With the publication of his review of the Edgeworths' *Readings on Poetry,* Dana came into his own as a romantic critic. The book, which provided a useful foil for another of his attacks upon Enlightenment ideas, was the product of a collaboration between the English educator Richard Edgeworth and his daughter Maria, a novelist and author of children's stories. The Edgeworths, who had won an international reputation for their contributions to primary school education, opposed the traditional reliance on rote learning. They recommended that children be taught general principles through practical exercises based on everyday experience.

While their work was unquestionably a step in the right direction, their application of Locke's psychological principles to poetry struck Dana as utterly misconceived. In addition to snatches of edifying poetry, *Readings on Poetry* contained commentaries designed to help little readers by defining words, explaining allusions, and providing useful information about the baking of bread and the tanning of leather. Such an approach to poetry, Dana complained, would produce "mere reasoning machines." It robbed poetry of its power to give "warmth and action to feelings" and to inspire a longing for the mysterious and exalted qualities of the human spirit.[32] "Miss Edgeworth would have her children clear-minded and sound reasoners," he wrote, "but she seems to have forgotten that they must first have imagination." He felt that it was a false and vicious system, one which, in the anxiety to protect children from passion and superstition, encouraged a "meaner servitude" to small-minded and selfish instincts. Anxious to make "matter-of-fact men of babes," the Edgeworths added little to the sum of children's knowledge while officiously getting in the way of their capacity to imagine, feel, and think for themselves.[33]

Perhaps memories of his own schoolboy miseries or his sympathy with Wordsworth's view of childhood persuaded Dana that each child's unique nature and personality were the best guide to his or her education. He believed that children should be encouraged to trust their emotions and instincts and to learn only what their curiosity dictated. The object of education, he insisted, is not knowledge but character—independence of spirit, ingenuity, courage, and sensitivity to beauty. In the work of the Edgeworths, "enough is not left to the workings of nature," he wrote. "With a vain and vulgar ignorance, we distrust the character she was silently and slowly moulding into beauty."[34] Nature should be a child's first teacher, and after nature, books of fantasy and natural history, like Aesop's fables, the *Arabian Nights,* and works describing peoples and cultures of foreign lands. At a time when some educators in America were urging a stricter emphasis upon classical training and others were counseling a greater stress on the useful, Dana's discussion of a child-centered program that stressed the importance of play, exercise, and nurturing of the imagination and spirit was original and innovative.

Dana suspected that the Edgeworths' book had been inspired, at least in part, by opposition to the educational ideas of transcendental metaphysicians. For why else would so much effort have been exerted to enthrone discursive reasoning and mindless fact gathering? Invoking Coleridge in his final rebuttal, Dana declared that true knowledge had other, higher sources: "imagination and words," he concluded, "*are* the highest metaphysicks."[35]

Dana's review of William Hazlitt's *Lectures on the English Poets* (1818) was his best critical piece to date and the one on which his reputation as a critic deservedly rests. In it Dana offered his fullest assessment of English poetry and tested his talents for literary criticism against one of the best romantic critics of his day. Like Dana, Hazlitt had been swept up in the revulsion against eighteenth-century rationalism. Hazlitt's earliest essays had been labored but intensely felt attempts to refute the philosophy that resolved all "thought into sensation, all morality into the *love of pleasure,* and all action into *mechanical* impulse."[36] The two men shared a number of basic ideas. Both claimed that the mind is an active agent in the creation of an individual's impressions of the world, and both believed that passions and feelings are sources of cognitive truths. They agreed, more or less, on the nature of the imagination and on the qualities that distinguish good poetry. As romanticists, they also shared a common enemy in the prestige accorded to the empirical method and to science. Hazlitt worried that the advances of science threatened to "demystify" the world, while Dana feared that the arrogance of scientific utilitarianism would lead to indifference, if not contempt, for the powers of imagination and intellect that defy quantification.

Despite these similarities, Dana frequently found himself at odds with Hazlitt. Although he admired Hazlitt's spirited and personal prose style, Dana believed that in his efforts to be "original and startling," Hazlitt was often partisan and inconsistent. Dana pointed to Hazlitt's treatment of Pope as an example of this inconsistency. After declaring that true poetry is marked by "imagination and passion, and an uneasy, restless sense of beauty," Hazlitt "presently . . . overtakes a man who has few or none of these qualities,—he is extremely intimate with him all of a sudden, and straightway turns round and contradicts all he had said before, and falls to abusing those who had gone peaceably along with him from the time he started. . . . He is a sort of Gonzolo, in poetry, and the latter part of his commonwealth is forever forgetting the beginning."[37] Hazlitt claimed that Pope was a "great writer of some sort," the unexcelled poet of personality and the polished life. This praise, however qualified, drove Dana into an uncharacteristic fury of indignation. Such an evenhanded appraisal of Pope seemed to him a betrayal of romantic critical standards. Dana was convinced that the American veneration of Pope was the single greatest obstacle to the writing of good poetry and to the acceptance of a romantic aesthetic. Pope may have been witty and ingenious, Dana conceded, but "he had no more idea of a poetical language than a Frenchman."[38] Convinced that he was taking on the entire Boston literary establishment, Dana drove his point home. Pope was no poet: his excessive use of antithesis, conceits, "unmeaning words," monotonous versification and rhyme schemes, false sentimentality, and misplaced passion disqualified him from the rank of a true poet.

Dana disagreed with Hazlitt, sometimes sharply, in his evaluation of other eighteenth-century poets. Hazlitt preferred Thomson to Cowper. In his judgment, Thomson was England's best descriptive poet because he conveyed the actual feel of nature without sacrificing unified impressions of the whole to the particularity of description. He dismissed Cowper as too fastidious and refined, a poet who shook hands with nature while keeping his gloves on. Dana, on the other hand, thought Thomson's descriptions of nature resembled "poetical maps of the world" or poetical "meteorological tables." He complained of Thomson's "unmeaning words," "cumbrous court-letter" diction, and indistinct personifications of things. He reminded Hazlitt that common words and simple, natural imagery have far more power to evoke associations of beauty than the Latinate language and set descriptions of Thomson. As for Cowper, Dana remarked, "it is hardly for Mr. Hazlitt, just let out from Pope's bandbox of ruffs and caps, to perk about in Cowper's fresh gravel-walks."[39] Dana recognized in Cowper a true lover of nature and admired his success in infusing natural scenes with religious and domestic sentiments. Most fundamentally, Dana's criticism of Hazlitt was that time and again he failed to honor the romantic standards of criticism that he had set down in his own introductory essay.

They disagreed, too, on the merits of George Crabbe. Hazlitt was bored and disgusted by Crabbe's descriptions of village life. Reading Crabbe, Hazlitt wrote, is like listening to the "old toothless, mumbling dame . . . doling out the gossip and scandal of the neighborhood." Crabbe is "the only poet who has attempted and succeeded in the *still life* of tragedy. . . . [He] seems to rely, for the delight he is to convey to his reader, on the truth and accuracy with which he describes only what is disagreeable."[40] Hazlitt complained that Crabbe's poetry dwelt upon only one emotion—unvarying, unrelieved gloom. Dana, however, admired the psychological realism of Crabbe's poetry. Deeply moved by "Peter Grimes," he felt that no poet since Shakespeare had succeeded as well as Crabbe in the vivid portrayal of a wide range of human character and experience. Dana's melancholy temperament might explain his admiration for Crabbe: what others considered a single chord, he perhaps experienced as a full orchestration of human emotions.

It was Hazlitt's cool appraisal of the work of Wordsworth and Coleridge that most outraged Dana, however. An admirer of the French Revolution and of Napoleon, Hazlitt could never forgive Wordsworth and Coleridge for renouncing their earlier revolutionary enthusiasm. Hazlitt accused Wordsworth of misapplying his fleeting libertarian principles to the realm of poetry: Wordsworth had dethroned elegance, metric beauty, and poetic diction with the same eagerness that he had once had for dethroning kings and queens. According to Hazlitt, Wordsworth made a principle out of poeticizing the commonplace, preferring the "meanest and most unpromising" of language and subject matter. Dana, who believed with Wordsworth that a special poetic diction was the folly of an artificial age, found it difficult to reconcile Hazlitt's romantic aesthetics with his lack of enthusiasm for Wordsworth and Coleridge. Ignoring, or perhaps unaware of, the political origins of Hazlitt's treatment of Wordsworth and Coleridge, Dana concluded that Hazlitt lacked the courage and independence of mind to praise what posterity had not yet sanctioned.[41] He also suspected Hazlitt of expressing opinions popular with the smart London crowd that circled about the British journalist and editor Leigh Hunt. Hazlitt, Dana wrote, is "too envious and spleeny, . . . too full of himself to have a sincere love and interest for what is abstractly good and great. . . . A dapper gentlemen he, who gets upon Parnassus, whips his boots with his rattan, and with a negligent twirl of it, cuts off the flowers smooth by the head."[42]

Of course Dana was not entirely free of partisanship himself, and was less than just when he accused Hazlitt of bowing to the ideas of his friends. Hazlitt was uncompromisingly honest, a man of independent mind and intense passions. In matching wits with Hazlitt, Dana had met a worthy opponent. If Dana had not always made the better argument, he had at least reasoned from consistent and clearly stated principles. If his prose was no match for Hazlitt's witty, memorable turns of phrase, it was at least muscular, clear, and direct. Dana had proved himself a perceptive and able critic.

Dana's review of Washington Irving's work was his most important contribution to the debate on literary nationalism and the last essay he was to write for the *North American Review*. In it he achieved an objectivity unusual for this period of nationalistic fervor. At a time when puffery was common, few American reviewers questioned the genius of Irving, the first native writer to win an enthusiastic readership at home and abroad. But Dana believed that Irving's talents could withstand scrutiny. Convinced that Irving was unlikely to become a writer of the first rank, yet confident that he would become one of America's "standard" authors, Dana argued that the *Sketch Book* was inferior to his earlier work. Irving's first stories were satires based on the history of New York and on the contemporary social scene. The *Sketch Book* drew on materials suggested by legends, folklore, and traditional customs. Dana believed that Irving had sacrificed vigor and spirit to subdued elegance in making the change from history to folklore. "We will be open with him," Dana wrote, "and tell him that we do not think the change is for the better." The earlier work was characterized by a gaiety, originality, and boisterous humor that Dana admired. Coming from a city where class and family pretensions and religious traditions made writers solemn and decorous, Dana envied Irving's New York, where social relations were freer and satire less resented. The *Salmagundi Papers* was "masculine—good bone and muscle," he wrote, "but the *Sketch Book* is feminine, *dressy,* elegant, and languid. . . . It is as if his mother English had been sent abroad to be improved, and in attempting to become accomplished, had lost too many of her home qualities."[43] With the exception of "Rip Van Winkle," which Dana admired for its "wild, mysterious, and visionary" atmosphere, the *Sketch Book* seemed less like a work heralding a new era in fiction than a throwback to the mannerisms, themes, and rhetorical style of the eighteenth century.

In Irving's work, Dana found some of the strengths and weaknesses noted earlier in the poetry of Washington Allston—purity of spirit, amiableness, sentimentality, and a flair for transforming the ludicrous into the picturesque. William Hedges, in his biography of Irving, asserts that Dana was the first of many critics to praise Irving's amiableness while underestimating the sharpness of his satire and the extravagance of his burlesque.[44] It is true that Dana stressed the "good feeling" behind the satire, praising the plausibility of character sketches while quoting, by way of illustration, from some of Irving's most absurd burlesques.

But Dana was from Boston. He believed that Irving's descriptions of New York were realistic, depicting "what was seen and felt," "present and real." Like most Bostonians, Dana was prepared to believe that a character like Will Wizard might be encountered on any street corner in New York, where people were the "most irregular, crazy-headed, quick-silver, eccentric, whim-whamsical set of mortals ever jumbled together." Amiability was certainly not one of the qualities Dana most admired. He much preferred satire, like Swift's, born from deeply felt grief at the world's heartlessness and mean selfishness. By Swift's standards, Irving's satire was, in fact, sweet-tempered. It was, as Dana suggested, the lightweight recreation of pleasant mornings and just the thing "in the rests between cotillions, and pauses between games of cards."[45]

The Bostonians Force a Resignation

The record of the immediate response to Dana's reviews has almost vanished: only a notice, cut from the pages of the *Federal Republic and Baltimore Telegraph,* remains to bear witness to a receptive audience. The author of this brief review singled out the *North American Review* as the most promising journal of the day and Dana's review of Hazlitt's *English Poets* as a piece worthy of the emerging literary character of the nation. He wrote that it was a "masterly article," which, "for beauty, propriety, originality of manner, and piquancy . . . is unequaled."[46] With characteristic self-deprecation, Dana scribbled the word "extravagant" in the margin.

Readers in the Boston area were, however, far less enthusiastic. The nineteenth-century anthologist Rufus Griswold recorded that "a strong party rose" against the opinions Dana had expressed in his reviews. Dana "had the whole influence of the university, of the literary and fashionable society of the city, and of the press to contend against."[47] When the first hints of this opposition surfaced, Dana refused to take it seriously. In a letter to his grandfather, he wrote:

Did [name crossed out] say that I was quite meek under the remarks of the
Bostonians upon my review? My meekness was indifference. I never cared a
fig for their opinion in matters of taste with regard to others, & am not quite
such a boy as to be troubled when they concern myself. This I know, that
what I said must have something in it, else they would not have talked so
long & so much & with so great heat about it. I know what Ned, [Edmund]
& the 'sacred few,' as I have elsewhere called them to the offending of the
many, think about it; & with that I always have & always shall rest satisfied
as concerns what I have done or may do.[48]

Despite this uproar, Dana confidently expected to be chosen the
next editor of the *North American Review;* but he underestimated the
strength of his critics and the timidity of the association of contributors whose fears for the circulation of the journal mounted with the
increasing furor. He told himself that the fuss was about his irrever-
ent attack on Pope, but he must surely have known that the issues
went deeper. He had, after all, challenged the conventional wisdom
of his day. He had raised questions about the adequacy of Scottish
commonsense philosophy, a set of ideas that dominated New England
thought until the middle of the century. He had said that Harvard
crushed genius and had accused the cultural custodians of encouraging
pedantry and entertaining a contempt for the tastes of ordinary people. In defending romantic aesthetics, he had thrown his weight behind a form of metaphysical idealism: he was, in short, guilty of that
most alarming of early nineteenth-century heresies—mysticism. To
suggest, as he had, that the private visions of the poet are truer than
the conventions of the community, and more imperative than social
solidarity, was simply unacceptable to Boston's "clerisy."

Dana paid the price for his courage and unorthodox opinions. The
association of contributors refused to make him the editor of the *Review.* When Channing resigned in 1819 to accept a professorship at
Harvard, they selected Edward Everett instead. Recognizing that the
election of Everett implied a repudiation of all that he stood for, Dana
withdrew from the association. The rejection of his bid for the editorship was a turning point not only for him but, in some sense, for the
literary and cultural life of Boston as well. With the departure of
Dana and Channing, the association added new members to their
ranks, men like Alexander Everett, John Gorham Palfrey, George
Ticknor, and William Prescott. Their tastes were cosmopolitan and
urbane but essentially conservative. Although they loved and encouraged literature, they valued balance, detachment, rationality, and

moderation more than originality and daring. Preferring that their authors be sociable men of equable temperaments, they distrusted solitary, brooding, and unreliable characters like Dana. These men took command of the cultural life of Boston for the next thirty years. Dana soon learned the truth about a remark made many years later by Henry Adams. In Massachusetts, Adams said, the union of church, bar, and respectable society created "an organized social system, capable of acting at command either for offence or defence, and admirably adapted for the uses of the eighteenth century."[49] The *North American Review* suffered from the forced resignation of Dana. William Cullen Bryant always insisted that if the *Review* "had remained in Dana's hands he would have imparted a character of originality and decision to its critical articles which no literary man of the country was at that time qualified to give it."[50]

A boyhood dream died when he was forced to resign from the *Review*. Since the days when his brother talked of the Monthly Anthology Society, Dana had wanted to be part of a community of like-minded literary men. He had even hoped, once appointed to the paying job of assistant editor, that he might make his living as a writer. All that seemed impossible without the editorial position. With a sense of shock, he realized that his opinions were not simply daring and unusual but unacceptable. His adversaries cast him in the role of the outsider, and, as time went by, the role became more congenial. The opposition of the Everetts, Nathan Hale, and others proved unrelenting. Dana never forgave them and believed, with good reason, that they did what they could to prevent his work from receiving a fair hearing. Although he subsequently would have ties with other periodicals, his role was never again as influential as it had been when he was with the *North American Review*. His later literary essays, though always interesting and original, lacked the confidence of his reviews of Hazlitt and Irving. In 1818 Dana had believed that he was in the vanguard only to discover that no one was following. Adversity, disappointments, and his own brooding personality converged to turn his imagination inward upon a claustrophobic landscape of dreams, frustrated passion, and guilt.

Chapter Three

The *Idle Man:* A Pilgrimage into Madness

The Founding of the *Idle Man*

Although deeply discouraged by the events which denied him the editorship of the *North American Review,* Dana did not give up. After learning of the unprecedented financial success of Irving's *Sketch Book,* he decided to bring out his own literary miscellany. In May 1821 the first number of the *Idle Man* was published. He chose the title as an ironic commentary on the low opinion that Americans had of professional writers. The six issues, published over a period of fifteen months, contained essays, fiction, a review of Edmund Keane's performance of *Richard III,* and poems by William Cullen Bryant and Washington Allston. Convinced that the mystery surrounding the authorship of the *Sketch Book* and Sir Walter Scott's *Waverley* novels had sparked public interest in those works, Dana too decided to write under a pseudonym. In an effort to conceal his identity from the unfriendly and "unimaginative critics" of Boston, he had the work printed in New York. Under arrangements made with the bookseller Charles Wiley, Dana paid the publication costs, a practice common at a time when publishing ventures by relatively unknown American authors were risky. The profits, if any, were to go to Dana to defray his costs.[1]

At first he was optimistic about the prospects for his work, especially when he detected approval among the "reading society" of Boston. The reviews of the first issues were generally favorable despite the unpopularity of his enthusiastic account of Keane's performance. Edmund Keane had enraged the theatergoers of Boston by walking out on a performance when he drew an audience of only twenty. But soon the *Idle Man* ran into problems. Shipments went astray and the costs of transportation and distribution were unexpectedly high: newspapers proved reluctant to print reviews and booksellers were slow to settle their accounts. Wiley kept Dana in a state of uncertainty about the future of the work, reporting discouraging sales while predicting eventual success and assuring him of the enthusiasm of discerning readers. Finally, readers began to fall away when Dana abandoned the sentimental stories of the first issues in favor of darker tales of violence and psychological anguish.

As a literary critic for the *North American Review*, Dana's task had been the relatively simple one of applying and defending a romantic aesthetic. When he attempted to translate his ideas into fiction of his own, he ran up against some of the problems inherent in the romantic perspective. Romanticists, or at least those influenced by Coleridge, were idealists who believed that the mind plays an active role in constructing the individual's experience of the world. Dana sensed that the great danger as well as the great attraction of romanticism lay in the idea that truth is not, as the Scottish realists claimed, a transcription of a reality existing externally but has its origins in the mind. The problem arose from the difficulty of establishing the validity of ideas so subjective in origin.

Dana's way of handling this dilemma in the tales written for the *Idle Man* went through a remarkable progression. In his earliest stories, he treated the imagination as a beautiful source of recreation in childhood and youth and as an innocent avenue of escape from an unfeeling and hostile world. Then, for a brief time, he subscribed to a form of transcendentalism. He wrote an essay suggesting that a wholly subjective rendering of experience can be trusted because the imagination is linked to a spiritual realm of being beyond the sensory phenomena of nature. In his last tale, the hero is carried by passion and imagination into a hell of madness and murder.

The implication, shocking to readers who liked his tender, sentimental tales, seemed to be that the imagination has no cosmic connections but merely projects upon nature the heart's desires and the disorders of the unconscious mind. When Dana wrote as if the imagination led to visions of beauty and a life of wholesome domesticity, the critics and readers applauded. When he explored the possibility that nihilism was the dark, reverse side of the romantic theory of the imagination, the critics were uncomprehending and outraged.

His journey through the metaphysical implications of romantic idealism was accompanied by an effort to find satisfactory literary forms. He floundered from one genre to another, seeking unsuccessfully for a style appropriate to what he had to say and congenial with his limited talents as a writer of fiction. Although Dana failed to

solve the problems of form and shuddered at the bleakness of his own
conclusions, his work did anticipate the possibilities and the dilemmas of the romantic vision.

Sentimental Essays and Stories

In his early pieces for the *Idle Man,* Dana drew heavily on the conventions of the sentimental novel.[2] The popularity of the genre appealed to him, for now that he was set upon making his living as a
writer, he did not want to risk offending his readers. The public's
appetite for sentimental stories was not his only reason for choosing
this form, however: he also found in it a way of expressing his hostility toward the emerging commercial order without seeming to attack
basic American values. His favorite theme was alienation. He was primarily interested in depicting the psychological anguish that overwhelmed young men of feeling and imagination (men like him) who
were forced to live in a world they could not love.

The theme of alienation was potentially quite radical. In the hands
of English and European romanticists, the alienated hero's dream of
freedom and his rage against autocratic rule, the brutality of industri-
alization, and the oppressiveness of social conventions challenged the
existing order. Dana's heroes, on the other hand, have no such focus
for their grief and anger. They do not openly attack the status quo.
They seem to exist, for the most part, outside of any specific economic or social context. They are troubled by those domestic trials
common to sentimental fiction—the death of a parent, the loss of an
inheritance, romantic love jeopardized by material dispossession.
These characters, however, often express feelings of isolation and dis-
affection that are disproportionate to their troubles. The heroes seem
inadequately motivated, a point contemporary critics sometimes
raised.

Dana had a very sophisticated understanding of the changes occur-
ring in America that were responsible for his own alienation. He recognized, for example, that a commercial market economy was
displacing an agrarian one, destroying both man's closeness to nature
and the hierarchical social order that nurtured communal obligations,
high culture, and traditional values; yet he did not attempt in any
sustained way to relate the alienation of his characters to these social
and economic issues. Perhaps he was afraid to attack a system that
Americans believed was the best in the world. The success of the

American republican experiment forced any writer in this country to treat the theme of alienation cautiously. To write stories suggesting that democracy and commercial growth were somehow responsible for the anguish and estrangement of his characters would be to abandon all hope of winning a sympathetic readership. Or more likely his own belief in the importance of strong social institutions made him loath to criticize even those of which he disapproved.

Sentimental fiction provided him with a literary strategy for reconciling his fascination with the outsider and his belief in the importance of community. It allowed him to express his lack of sympathy for the new order without risking public disapproval. This genre, which gained popularity in the 1820s, served to rationalize the new system of assigning work by gender, which accompanied the development of the market economy. Many of the productive tasks formerly done in the home by women—brewing, baking, weaving, candle-making—were absorbed into a commercial nexus. The world of work, at least for middle-class urban Americans, was divided into two spheres. Men labored outside the home while women were assigned the responsibility of caring for the children and preserving moral and spiritual values that were thought irrelevant in the impersonal marketplace. Sentimental fiction was popular because it exalted this new role for women. Dwelling on the special emotional and spiritual qualities peculiar to women, this genre depicted the home as a sanctuary of goodness, piety, and virtue in a world dominated by the ruthless considerations of the market. This morally polarized view of the world suited Dana's purposes exactly. He endowed his heroes with the qualities of mind and heart valued most in the domestic sphere. In the home and in the company of women, his heroes discover an atmosphere in which they can freely express their disgust over a social and economic order that is at odds with their deepest feelings. His heroes are not necessarily reformed by women, which was the usual psychological dynamics depicted in the sentimental domestic novel. Instead they find in female companionship the freedom to be who they truly are. By ascribing feminine virtues to his heroes, Dana could censure a society that asked men to sacrifice their higher impulses to the business of making money. Although critics might accuse him of being unworldly, they could not say that he was either radical or unpatriotic.

In "Domestic Life," one of his early essays for the *Idle Man,* Dana suggested that in this polarized world of work and home, the man who lives without the redemptive influence of wife and family risks having his imagination and power of feeling destroyed by cynicism and despair. He began his essay by drawing a contrast between youth, when the imagination is the dominant influence, and adulthood, when reality holds sway. For a brief time, he wrote, all is a "wonder and delight to us"; then the veil lifts, reality intrudes, and faith and feeling are checked. He believed that a man's future hangs on this moment when reality first seriously challenges the imagination, for then he faces several choices. He may put aside his youthful dreams and become wise, prudent, and complacent and play the world's game. Or he may become a moral outlaw—a man in the mold of Byron's Manfred—who frees himself from social conventions. Moved by dreams of higher truth, he may defy the decencies and rules that guide more ordinary, or more ambitious, men. Or he may choose to live the life of the *isolato,* disappointed and estranged by the disparity between what is and what his imagination tells him might be. Or, if he is lucky, he will find a safe harbor in domestic happiness. That Dana found his categories convincing and the suggested responses sympathetic is born out by the fact that he wrote about each of these character types in the *Idle Man.*

He believed that the home is the only setting in which the imagination can flourish on into adulthood and the feelings of disappointment and estrangement can be translated into love. In the company of children, a man's imagination keeps its sweetness and innocence. The anger he feels at the injustice and cruelty in the world loses its harshness when it arises out of love for his family. In the last analysis, of course, it is a woman who, in this sentimental scheme of things, prevents the "virtuous tendencies of . . . youth" from running into vice. Out of love for her, Dana wrote, a man learns to value his feelings above "mere intellect." She leads him from physical passion to beatitude: a man finds that after a few years "his relish for the grosser pleasures is lessened, and that he has grown into a fondness for the intellectual and refined without an effort, and almost unawares. He has been led onto virtue through his pleasures."[3] Dana felt that only in the roles of husband and father could a man receive social approval for his sensitivity, moral longings, and idealism. Expressions of joy and grief, which would be thought inappropriate in the worldly male sphere, could be shown openly in the sanctuary of the home. Familial responsibilities would elevate his efforts to "succeed," efforts that might seem tainted or ignoble if not undertaken in the service of those he loves. In the home, Dana wrote, "We are put into a right relation with the world; neither holding it in proud scorn, like the solitary man, nor being carried along by . . . vague and careless notions of things, like the world's man."[4]

In an essay, "Letter from Town," Dana tried to dramatize a conversation between two men of the world. Composed in the epistolary style of eighteenth-century essays, his attempt at brisk and worldly repartee was undercut by an incongruous moral earnestness. He patterned the character of Abraham, one of the patrons of the tavern, on the successful, prudent, and down-at-the-mouth citizens of Boston. Abraham robs his children of the joys of childhood and his wife of sympathetic companionship by treating life as a trial and an affliction. Tom, on the other hand, is equally guilty of destroying domestic happiness but for opposite reasons. Self-indulgent and carefree, he observes the "two-sphere" principle to a fault. He sees his wife only when they dine out or entertain at home, leaves all household responsibilities in her hands, and teaches his sons to enjoy life by setting them the example of a tavern habitué. In their narrow selfishness, both Abraham and Tom deny themselves the moral and spiritual benefactions of domestic life.

Dana's first fictional exploration of the intimate emotions of domestic life was in the insubstantial story entitled "The Son." The story, which is a tribute to filial love and a meditation on the conflicting emotions that accompany grief, was probably based on his memories of his mother's death. In it he also tried for the first time to describe the experiences and feelings of one whose life is governed by the imagination. The main character, Arthur, is a thoughtful, solitary, and dreamy young man whose domestic affections provide "substantiality" to his visions and are his only anchor to the real world. Because Dana had rejected, for the moment, the greater literary possibilities offered by the characters of the *isolato* and the Byronic hero, he went to some lengths to elevate his man of feeling to the status of a hero. In his preface to the story, he advised his readers that Arthur, who might have seemed to some almost effeminate in his emotionality, is possessed of a moral grandeur. Dana argued that the delicacy and refinement shown by the man who is "borne along by the delightful and kind affections of private life," are more compelling demonstrations of character than the heroic gestures of men called upon to make sacrifices in the name of great principles. The first "falls in with the order of nature, which is grounded in truth" while the heroism of the second is no guarantee against coarseness and insensitivity.[5] He defined virtue as taking "the easy way of the better propensities of our nature." This sentiment may have been appealing to some, but it offered only limited fictional possibilities—not to mention its ethical and moral vacuousness.

In "The Son," Dana gave a detailed description of the progression of grief—the first tumultuous anguish, the sense of loss, awe, and reverence, the numb insensibility, and the final resignation and tranquility. His closely observed modulation of feelings and his sustained tone of melancholy made the story popular with both critics and the public; however, without plot, character development, or close social observation, the story offered little evidence of narrative or dramatic power.

Dana's second story, "Edward and Mary," is the melodramatic tale of a romance nearly doomed by a lost inheritance. The work is interesting primarily because it is his first attempt to depict the transforming power of the imagination. The hero of the story, Edward Shirley, is a grave, solitary young man who holds himself apart from the society around him out of the conviction that he will never find true happiness. Sensitive and idealistic, Edward feels repelled by the thought of having to make his way in the hard world of his father's business. He "had read so much of wrong, and had learned to think that there was so little of true delicacy and deep and enduring love amongst men to answer to what he felt within himself, that he was sensible of something like a distaste for the world at large."[6]

Edward Shirley lives largely within his imagination, seeking pleasure and companionship in the beauty of woods and fields. Communion with nature cannot satisfy the longings of the sentimental hero, however. "We are made for other purposes," Dana wrote, "than to have our interests begin and end" in nature.[7] Although sensitive to its spiritual undertones, Edward's only hope of a true communion with life lies not in the redemptive power of nature but in the romantic love and security of domestic life. He finds this love when he meets the beautiful Mary Aston; but before he can avow his love and propose marriage, his father is bankrupted by unwise speculations. Because Edward is too honorable to ask Mary to share his uncertain future, the lovers part, believing that they will never see each other again. This tragedy is averted when an old family friend gives Edward a generous annuity, enabling him to buy back the family estate. The lovers then marry and presumably live happily ever after.

The sentimental plot of the story interested Dana less than the opportunity it provided him for describing the imagination. Dana's real accomplishment was to show how the intensified emotions of the lover lend an energy to the imagination, which, like that of the Romantic artist, projects onto nature an imagined significance. In words that seem to allude to the disappointment and bitterness of his own postponed marriage, Dana remarked, "Thwarted love is more romantic than even that which is blessed." Under its influence "the imagination grows forgetive, and the mind idles, in its melancholy, among fantastic shapes; all it hears or sees is turned to its own uses, taking new forms and new relations, and multiplying without end; and it wanders off amongst its own creations, . . . till it loses sight of the world."[8]

After meeting Mary for the first time, Edward discovers that "nature gives him a new delight." When he learns of his father's financial losses, nature seems transformed: trees and flowers that had given him so much pleasure only weeks before now appear to be "the emblems of his own withered joys." Returning to claim Mary as his bride, he feels that nature shares in his joy. Dana described the moment: "The raindrops were falling from the trees like pearls, . . . the brooks ran shining on, prattling like young living things noisy with joy. Everything upon the earth seemed in action, and he felt as if there was a spirit of motion within him, bearing him forward."[9] By placing the source of these sentiments within Edward's heart, Dana avoided the worst emotional excesses of the pathetic fallacy. He admitted in a letter to Bryant, however, that "Edward and Mary" was "not much of a story neither—just enough to hang some of our feelings upon."[10]

As the popularity of the lavishly illustrated gift annuals demonstrated, the reading public demanded just this sort of sentimental trifle. A reviewer for the *Columbian Centinel* thought it "a beautiful little book." "It is," the reviewer wrote, "rich in sentiment, full of nervous, brilliant language, playful and graceful expression, and vivid thoughts."[11] Another critic for the same newspaper praised Dana's indifference to the popular demand for uniformity, adding that he had succeeded in "striking out something after his own fashion."[12] The critic for the *Boston Weekly Messenger* noted some "peculiar humours" in Dana's work but reassured readers that, on the whole, the *Idle Man* contributed to the spirit of morality and the improvement of public taste.[13] In a letter to William Cullen Bryant, Dana expressed amusement at his growing reputation as a "charming, sentimental man, & such a lover." He observed, even "a black hen may lay a white egg."[14]

For a short time, the sentimental story suited Dana's purposes. Its popularity ensured him an audience while allowing him to depict the alienated man of feeling in an appealing light. Dana soon began to lose interest in the genre, however, partly because he had doubts about his ability to write such stories and partly because he saw greater possibilities in tales depicting the psychology of the Byronic hero and the *isolato*. After writing "Edward and Mary," Dana admitted to Bryant, "I'm not at all clever at a story. I wish I were, it is always so popular & taking, & so it should be."[15] He also sensed that while the domestic affections were vital to the well-being of a man and a nation, they were perhaps not rich enough to sustain serious fiction. Toward the end of his essay "Domestic Life," he had written: "I have thought that I could talk of it for ever. It is not so. Though the feeling of home never wearies, . . . yet the feeling itself, and that which feeds it, have a simplicity and unity of character of which little is to be told."[16]

In his next essay, "Musings," and in his last two stories for the *Idle Man,* Dana began to explore the further implications of Coleridge's theory of the imagination. He only needed to develop ideas in "Edward and Mary" to raise some interesting, even disturbing, possibilities. For one thing, might not Edward's egoistic self-absorption, while merely a prelude to love and a meaningful reentry into the human community, lead in other circumstances to actions destructive of community? What of the encounter between the individual's imagination and nature? Did it simply provide, as in "Edward and Mary," an enhanced sense of self, or was it perhaps a way of discovering in the symbol-rich surface of nature a deeper spiritual reality? Dana surprised his readers, and maybe himself, when in his next essay he moved from yet another description of the alienated man of feeling into an evocation of this transcendental vision.

"Musings" begins with a description of the twofold life of the man of feeling. Such a man goes about his affairs, appearing to others to be no different from them. But his deeper passions, more acute sensations, and livelier imagination place him at odds with those whose hearts have been hardened by greed and whose concern with the utility of nature has defrauded them of its spiritual significance. While these men calculate the monetary value of the lumber in a forest and the tillable soil lying beneath lakes and marshes, the man of feeling sees everything through the transforming eye of the imagination. Dana wrote: "In the man of feeling and imagination [everything] lays by its particular and short-lived and irregular nature, and puts on the garments of spiritual beings, and takes the everlasting nature of the soul. . . . All that his mind falls in with, it sweeps along in its deep, and swift, and continuous flow, and bears onward with the multitude that fill its shoreless and living sea."[17] Although this two-fold life sets him apart from the multitude, it may also provide "healings for a wounded mind," and consolation for "pain and poverty and the world's neglect."[18]

If, however, the imagination offers only consolation and if the answering spirit in nature is but a poetic fancy, the transcendental position would be an illusion. In the second part of "Musings," Dana tried to address this issue. His handling of this question was ambiguous, as it was for most romanticists. On the one hand, he believed that the imagination imparts highly personal and subjective meanings to nature. On the other hand, he recognized that if, as Coleridge had suggested, the imagination arises out of the soul and shares with nature an identical origin in one and the same spiritual reality, then the imagination may express universal, even divine, truths. In "Musings," he wrote an eloquent defense of this second position.

When the imagination contemplates nature, Dana reasoned, the age-old dualism separating the self from the world is healed. The "man of fine feeling and . . . deep creative thought" who approaches nature with the simplicity of a child will find an "answering spirit in everything."[19] In the intensity of this unifying experience, the polarity of subject and object, soul and body, mind and spirit dissolves. Dana described the experience: "Soul and body are blending into one; the senses and thoughts mix in one delight; he sees a universe of order and beauty, and joy and life, of which he becomes a part, and finds himself carried along in the eternal going-on of nature."[20]

No longer distressed by the apparent triumph of evil over good or by the tragedy of pain and death, the man of feeling sees a fitness, order, and beauty that "frees him from the formalities of rule, and lets him abroad to find a pleasure in all things, and order becomes a simple feeling of the soul. . . . He moves among the bright clouds; he wanders away into the measureless depths of the stars, and is touched by the fire with which God has lighted them."[21] Dana's belief in the identity between the poet's imagination and the divine fire linked his "Musings" with Coleridge's *Biographia Literaria*. This faith inspired his remarkable affirmation of the poet's freedom to take pleasure in all things and to write without concern for prescribed rules.

"Musings" not only was the first statement of the transcendental position by an American but also marked the end of Dana's cordial relations with readers and critics. Soon after its publication, Dana heard from Willard Phillips of strong opposition mounted by a "clan of young men in town" who had declared that his work "ought not to go."[22] In an essay written for the *North American Review*, a spokesman for the group, William H. Prescott, complained that Dana's "Musings" was an example of a new kind of metaphysical speculation, characterized by "mystical, fine-spun, indefinite phraseology whose object seems to be, rather to conceal thought, than to express it."[23] In later years such charges would be made against Emerson, Alcott, and other transcendentalists. Like Dana they too would find it difficult to express their visionary idealism in the precise, logical terms demanded by the men of the *Review*. Although Dana did not write again in this transcendental vein, it is unlikely that he was intimidated by the outcry. Despite the apparent confidence and boldness of his essay, he was moving into a period of doubt and soul-searching in which the issue of the imagination's subjectivity posed questions that he felt helpless to answer. If he did not go forward into transcendentalism, he did not retreat into sentimental fiction either. He pursued instead the darker fates of the Byronic outlaw and the *isolato*.

Outlaw and *Isolato*

Dana's next story, "Thomas Thornton," was a tale of murder, madness, and adventure on the high seas. The action-filled plot was something of a subterfuge, however, because for Dana the challenge of writing the story was in describing a psychological process of moral and spiritual disintegration. As his early pieces suggest, he was intrigued by the journey of youth from innocence to experience and by what becomes of the wonderfully promising qualities of youth— imagination, moral feelings, bravery, and idealism—when the real world imposes its conflicting demands. The theme had Byronic overtones, and Thornton resembles one of Byron's heroes in superficial ways. He has crisp black hair, a swarthy complexion, fiery eyes, and a manly, open countenance. Thornton is handsome, passionate, proud, and brave. The similarity ends there, however, because Dana's attempt to create a character like Byron's outlaws trapped him in insoluble contradictions. His own alienation from American society enabled him to write sympathetically about the feelings of such outcasts. At the same time, his political conservatism, his belief that men are truly human only within a well-defined social order, led him to conceal, if not wholly deny, the social and political origins of his character's rage. As a result, Thornton's anger is unfocused, his character unconvincing.

In "Thomas Thornton," the egotism and self-absorption that had seemed so innocent a part of Edward's character in "Edward and Mary" are cast in a more troubling light. Thornton's courage, pride, and reckless bravado make him a leader of his schoolmates in mischief and vandalism. After a brawl with his schoolmaster, Tom defies his father by refusing to apologize and leaves home. He announces to his mother, "I am a rebel and an outlaw," and to his father, "I will do something to [win myself a reputation] if I hang for it. I'll not lead a milksop life of it, to be called respectable by old women, young sycophants, and moneylenders."[24] Before signing up for a sea voyage, Tom visits an old school friend, Isaac Beckford. Beckford is the typical villain of nineteenth-century melodrama. A sly, vicious man consumed by envy of Tom's handsome figure and quick mind, Beckford plots to ruin him. Like Carwin in Charles Brockden Brown's *Wieland,* Beckford uses whatever intelligence he has to manipulate others; unlike Carwin's, Beckford's wickedness is not mitigated by the forcefulness of his mind or the noble ends at which his acts are aimed.

Seafaring life suits Tom's passionate nature. In six years he rises to second in command. When he returns from the sea, he succumbs to an uncontrollable desire for Beckford's distant cousin, the vain, beautiful, and ambitious Mrs. Fanny Henley,. Her marriage bores her, and she goes along with Beckford's plan to destroy Tom for her own reasons. Ignoring the pleas of his parents and the advice of his friends, Tom becomes the slave of his more violent passions. He drinks, gambles, duels, falls into debt, and recklessly presses his attentions upon Fanny. Only the death of his father and the suspicions of Mr. Henley save Tom from adultery. Chastened by guilt and remorse, Tom vows to mend his ways and goes again to sea; but he cannot forget his desire for Mrs. Henley. When he returns two years later, he vows to have her "come on't what may." Because she is now a widow, his ambition is quickly realized. But soon he wearies of the "high life" and of his role as an "ornament and a help to notoriety." He realizes that Fanny's beauty, high spirits, and intelligence are no substitute for delicacy of feeling, principles, and a fond heart. Dis-

gusted with his new life and racked by guilt over the neglect of his
widowed mother, Tom is easily led by Beckford into another round
of drinking and gambling. After he steps in to avert Thornton's
bankruptcy, Beckford claims Fanny's sexual favors as his reward.
When Tom discovers that Beckford has shamed, cuckolded and betrayed him, he kills him. Because Beckford's body is never found, the
murder goes undetected. Tom is imprisoned for debt, however.
While in prison he learns that his mother is dying. Already dis-
traught over the murder, he is finally driven mad by the burden of
guilt, remorse, and grief. Upon his release, he seeks refuge in an
abandoned seaman's shanty on the New England coast where he lives
off shellfish and is visited only by the specter of Fanny, who calls to
him from just beyond the "growling surf." Finally he dies, but not
before repenting his sins and making his peace with God.

Despite the obvious triteness and melodramatic quality of the plot,
Dana's "Thomas Thornton" is superior in several ways to any fiction
that he had yet written. The dialogue is more natural and colloquial
than in his earlier work. Several scenes, especially those that describe
the New England coast, were written with an eye for detail and a
sensitivity to tone. His brisk, economic prose style contrasts sharply
with the showy, Latinate prose of many of his contemporaries; but
Dana still had not given much thought to the special craftsmanship
demanded in short fiction. Twists of plot and a profusion of characters
more appropriate to the novel are crammed into the space of a short
story. It is not surprising that Dana complained to Bryant: "In telling
a story I've not room to turn around."[25]

To compare Tom Thornton with other outlaw-heroes in European
and English romantic fiction is to be struck by the shallowness of
Dana's conception. Thornton's egotism and defiance amount to nothing more than boyish bravado. The injustices against which he rages
are not the vast injustices of state and God that enraged the heroes
created by Byron, but are only the petty tyrannies of father and
schoolmaster. Thornton's reckless slide into degradation and madness
are not motivated by some Faustian hunger for knowledge and experience but only by weakness of character. When compared to the cosmic rage of Byron's heroes, Thornton's defiance seems peculiarly
unmotivated. Dana does offer interpretations, but these hardly measure up to the claim Thornton makes for himself: Thornton is neither
a rebel nor an outlaw.

Dana's confusion and hesitations are apparent from the several contradictory explanations that he offered for Thornton's behavior and character. At moments Dana implied that society was too tame, artificial, and corrupt for a man of Thornton's headstrong and adventurous nature. At other times he undercut this explanation by introducing the notion, widely accepted among moralists of the day, that antisocial behavior was the consequence of disordered moral faculties. Dana suggested that Thornton's reason, will, and feelings were unbalanced by the discordant attitudes of his parents. His mother is permissive and weak; his father is stern and tyrannical. As a result, Thornton despises his mother and fears his father, does as he pleases, and loses "all distinction of principle in self-gratification." To these social and psychological theories, Dana added a third. At times he described Thornton as a man driven by compulsions that defy rational interpretation. For no clear reason, Tom seems recklessly bent on self-destruction. In the end Dana fell back upon the Calvinisitic observation that Thornton "is a creature of sin."

Dana's inconsistency is not the issue here. The question is why he failed to draw more fully upon his own understanding of the social basis of alienation. Disgusted by the materialism, mediocrity, and antisocial self-interest he saw all around him, Dana might have crafted a story that made sense of Thornton's resentment and despair. Instead he reduced the social issue to a moral and psychological one. His failure was not simply literary but arose from his inability to reconcile the tension between the individual and society. A wholehearted acceptance of the values of society seemed to him unworthy of a man, but a life lived outside or in defiance of the community seemed to invite some terrible extinction of the self.

James Fenimore Cooper, whose view of these issues was less stark than Dana's, created characters who did effectively raise the social issue that troubled Dana. In *The Pioneers,* the values of the community and the principles of the solitary man are pitted against each other, and against the materialistic and wasteful culture. Of course, Cooper was a better storyteller than Dana, but their differences went beyond talent. Cooper understood that the tension, although it had a bearing on his private life, was not a personal problem but one with historic roots and broad social, demographic, and cultural causes.

Dana, on the other hand, experienced these tensions as a personal failing. Since adolescence he had felt that he was born out of his time. He tended to internalize the conflict between his commitment to the life of the community and his sense of personal alienation, accusing himself of possessing a character and talent ill-suited to the age. A growing interest in orthodox Christianity appears to have added weight to his belief that responsibility for social estrangement and disorder must be borne by the sinful individual. As a result, he was lured more and more deeply into psychological explanations of the imagination, explanations that divorced the poet-visionary from both nature and society.

The spring of 1822 was a time of deep personal crisis for Dana. His wife died of tuberculosis and his infant daughter died a short time later from the effects of a fall. His loss was great, for his marriage had been a happy one. His accounts of the attractions of domestic life were based not only on the popular sentimental stereotype but also on his own tender relationship with Ruth Charlotte. His son Richard later wrote that his mother's death had caused his father a grief "which no description of agony short of madness has equalled."[26] Dana reported to Bryant that every time he set pen to paper, "some tho't of what had past [sic] would come up in my mind . . . & its power over me was terrible & beyond all control—it swept me away like a flood. . . . Such was my dread of the effects of writing upon me that I shrunk from it as a man would from thrusting his hand into the fire."[27] Already despondent over the shift in critical opinion and the poor sales of the issue containing the Thornton story, Dana seems to have been carried by his distress to the brink of insanity.

The story he wrote during this period, "Paul Felton," clearly bears the marks of this emotional turmoil. He abandoned the story during the period of his most intense mourning, resuming it again in the early summer. "Paul Felton" was a kind of catharsis, written "with more rapidity & ease" than anything he had yet written.[28] In the story, he came to terms with the two unresolved questions of the *Idle Man* period. First, the story contains his only unambiguous treatment of the problem of alienation. Paul's estrangement from the human community is not presented as a self-protective response to the unacceptable corruptions of the world but as a manifestation of a deep psychological disturbance. Second, the imagination, which he had represented in "Musings" as a power capable of bringing the individual to an understanding of the spiritual ground of being, is treated in "Paul Felton" as the unreliable faculty that objectifies the delusions of madness.

Paul Felton is a young man in whom the ordinary conflicts within the human psyche have become exaggerated, overmastering forces.

Raised by a widowed father on an isolated country estate, he has grown up with books, nature, and his own thoughts for companions. Paul is moody, reserved, and not at all handsome. As a result of his solitude, he is filled with self-doubts and suspicion, and tormented by the conviction that he will never escape his loneliness or inspire love and sympathy in another. Dana remarked that "the love of what is excellent may lead us astray." So it is with Felton, whose anxiety about the accomplishments and virtues he lacks is inspired by his admiration of the good; yet the knowledge of his own weaknesses poisons his spirit with envy and hatred. Self-distrust and solitude have "set all at war and in opposition in his character" until at last "his mind seemed given for little else than to speculate upon his feelings, to part or unite them, or to quell them only again to inflame them."[29] Dana depicts his character as a romanticist. He says of Felton: "To him [nature] was a grand and beautiful mystery,—in his better moments, a holy one. It was power, and intellect, and love, made visible, calling out the sympathies of his being, and causing him to feel the living Presence throughout the whole. Material became intellectual beauty with him; he was as a part of the great universe, and all he looked upon, or thought on, was in some way connected with his own mind and heart."[30]

This vision is a fleeting one, however, for on many occasions Paul's spirit is in such discord that communion with nature is denied him. Then, when he sought the living Presence in nature, "imploring to be taken to a share of the joy," she "heard him not."[31] Readers familiar with the conventions of romantic literature would have recognized immediately that this alienation from nature is an omen of Felton's tragic fate.

The same self-distrust and moral ambivalence that deny Paul the blessings of nature also stand between him and the joys of domestic life. His love for Esther Waring cannot free him from his isolation because he cannot believe that she truly loves him. Her beauty, grace, and vivaciousness, the very qualities that first inspired his love, also arouse his suspicions. He reasons that Esther cannot care for him if she is so unlike him and so delighted in the company of people whose backgrounds and accomplishments are so different from his own. In the months after their marriage, his emotions become increasingly erratic. At one moment, he perceives that all of his best feelings have been liberated and are "taking the hues and forms of all the beautiful and blessed things with which God has filled the earth for us." At the next moment, his mind becomes abstracted with premonitions of betrayal and tragedy. All his doubts become certainties when he sees his wife dancing with a former suitor and overhears insinuations about her unhappiness in their "Vulcan and Venus" match. Soon violent and uncontrollable passions that seem like "powers independent of his will" gain mastery over Paul. He becomes convinced that he is possessed by demonic forces that command him to kill his wife, and he does so. Momentarily recovering his sanity, he realizes the enormity of what he has done and the shock kills him.

Dana's primary interest in "Paul Felton"—the challenge that aroused him from the despair and lethargy brought on by his wife's death—was in describing the progression of feelings and sensations that might accompany the process of going mad. He thought of insanity as a war within the personality, a battle between the forces of good and evil for the possession of the soul. Dana depicts Paul as undergoing emotional conflicts so intense that he feels as if his physical form is being altered. He used the metaphor of demonic possession to represent what we today would call paranoid schizophrenia. The metaphor is not in itself troubling for it would be difficult to think of a better one at a time when schizophrenia was not understood. But Dana used this device in a clumsy, melodramatic way. To dramatize this theme of possession, he introduced into the plot an insane boy named Abel who is both the horrified spectator of Felton's seizures and the voice of the demonic presence. Abel is constantly begging Felton to release him from his bondage or skipping crazily about on the ridges of neighboring hills. The reader is not made a witness to the progression of Felton's madness through descriptions of his behavioral changes but is plunged, instead, into Felton's mind amid too much shrieking and tearing of hair. The accounts of Felton's seizures—the descriptions of leering faces, monstrous forms, and fanged demons—resemble scenes from Heironymous Bosch's *Last Judgment*. Such images were appropriate enough in the fifteenth century but were likely to appear overdone in the less literal-minded nineteenth century.

Dana's failure to exert effective control over his materials and to devise less archaic ways of representing madness reveal the limitations of his talent as a writer of fiction. These failures also reflect his growing misgivings about the imagination. At one time he had thought of the poet or man of feeling as having a special relationship with nature and God. In "Paul Felton," however, Dana suggested that, although all of us are closer to madness than we know, it is just such individuals, those with the greatest intelligence, imagination, and sensitivity, who are most likely to go mad. He was not referring to "divine madness," either. He wrote:

There are souls who have hours of bright and holy aspirations, when they feel as if nothing of earth or sin could touch them more; but in the midst of their clear and joyous calm they feel some dark and frightful passion, like an ugly devil, beginning to stir within them. Their minds try to fly from it, but, as if it saw its hour, it seizes on its prey with a fanged hold, and there is no escape. Perhaps there are no minds of the highest intellectual order, that have not known moments when they would have fled from thoughts and sensations which they felt to be like visitants from hell.[32]

In the poetry of Wordsworth and Coleridge, Dana had once seen evidence that the imagination is a source of spiritual truth. In "Musings" he had argued that there exists an identity between the imagination and the spiritual ground of being that validates our trust in our own intuitions. But in "Paul Felton," he abandoned this transcendental faith, suggesting instead that the imagination is subordinate to the unconscious mind and therefore capable of reflecting only the state of a person's soul. Dana's doubts about the imagination are apparent in a passage in which Felton defends his belief that the imagination perceives intimations of God's love and perfection in nature. Felton's argument is unconvincing, however, because only moments before, he had sworn that evil spirits are at work in the world. Torn between these two conflicting views, Felton asks, "Are there not passing in and around this piece of moving mould, in which the spirit is pent up, those whom it hears not? . . . Are all the instant joys [and terrors] that come and go, we know not whence or whither, but creations of the mind?"[33] Although Felton promptly rejects this notion, the story supports it. The good and evil perceived in nature have the same status: both are figments of the imagination. The recognition that the imagination is wholly subjective, declaring only human truths, had tremendous literary possibilities for those unafraid to face the limitations of our humanity. For Dana it raised only the terrifying specter of nihilism. Increasingly convinced that humanity is inherently evil, he believed that the ability to know truth and to feel a kinship with nature depends upon a power higher than the individual.

The Fate of the *Idle Man*

A deeply felt and nearly unanimous outcry followed the publication of "Paul Felton." Readers complained that Felton's feelings and actions seemed inexplicable—his "mighty mind" had no object grand enough to justify his torment. They were offended by the pessimistic view of human nature implied in the story, fearing that the tale would encourage misanthropy and a disgust for society. "Well Wisher," writing for the *Columbian Centinel,* wondered "for what reason these unnecessary developments of the mysteries of the human soul are made. The mass of readers take little interest in the mysterious workings of such minds and upon those who do, an unjurious effect is produced."[34]

Dana was convinced by his treatment at the hands of the editors of the *North American Review* that he would never receive a fair hearing from Boston's cultural standard bearers. The editors chose William Cullen Bryant to review the *Idle Man.* When Bryant expressed his admiration of the work, the editors demanded substantial revisions, advising Bryant that he had "praised The Idle Man *plus quam satis* and more than would go down."[35] Dana wrote Bryant explaining that the editors sought to "garble your review—retain all the objections you make, & take out some of the praise, & so make you say what you never intended." Dana added that if the editors insisted upon these changes, he would prefer that no review be published at all, "for that would indeed be a clever way, for my enemies to make a thrust at me thr' my friends."[36] (In 1828 the *North American Review* finally printed an abbreviated version of Bryant's essay as part of a review of Dana's poetry.) Bryant commiserated with Dana over the injustice of such concerted opposition to his work: "I did not indeed feel altogether certain that it would be admitted, from what I knew of the opposition made to you by some of those concerned in the *North American Review,* but when I thought of the praises sometimes lavished by that work on productions which your most strenuous opposers could not think for a moment of putting in comparison with yours, I must confess I hardly expected it would be refused admission."[37]

Unwilling to ignore critics' misrepresentation of Dana's work, Bryant wrote a reply to "Well Wisher." To the charge that the Felton story was a covert attack on society, one that cast solitude and melancholy in an attractive light, Bryant pointed to the obvious fact that solitude, not society, had encouraged Paul's insanity. The story, Bryant argued, illustrates that both solitude and society have an equally unfortunate effect on a diseased mind. As for the hue and cry over the influence such stories would have on readers, Bryant commented, "To the sound mind they can do no harm, and he who is predisposed to insane wandering, would extract melancholy, I suppose, from a description of Adam and Eve in Paradise."[38]

The *North American Review* had earlier published an essay by William Prescott that contained a brief notice of the first four numbers of the *Idle Man*. The Augustan outlook of the old *Monthly Anthology* conservatives lived on in Prescott. He detected in the *Idle Man* many symptoms of a general decline in culture. Prescott complained not only of the vague and mystical speculations in "Musings," but also of a style and language that disregarded the rules and standards set by the masters of the eighteenth century. Damning Dana with faint praise, Prescott expressed some enthusiasm for the sentimental stories, especially for "The Son," which he thought the best piece in the first four issues. Stories about alienated heroes, Prescott remarked, bore witness to a personality "morbidly alive to such little troubles as most men would shake off in the eagerness of worldly occupation."[39] His comment is a revealing one. Prescott and his allies among the Everett/Hale circle had no sympathy with romanticism and, if possible, even less understanding of the lofty estrangement so often felt by its proponents.

The *Idle Man* came to an end with the publication of "Paul Felton." Dana had failed in his attempt to make his living as a professional writer. Stung by the unfavorable remarks of critics and especially by his treatment at the hands of the editors of the *North American Review,* and bled by slow sales into a debt of three hundred dollars, he had not the heart to go on. Among the Dana Papers is an undated fragment of a letter in which he started to explain why his career as a writer of fiction had aborted:

if it be asked how it is that I have produced so little, all I feel inclined to reply is, if The Idle Man had succeeded, I have no doubt I should have gone on in my literary labours, & have been a somewhat voluminous writer by this time; or that had I felt independent of the world in my circumstances, failure of success in that undertaking would not have stopt [*sic*] me. I could not say more without going into an account of my internal state, wh' after all another would not understand, & wh' I should not be inclined to do even if he could. When—[40]

The fragment ends abruptly as if Dana could not bear to recall this internal state. He alluded, of course, to the grief and mental discord brought on by his wife's death. For several years after the ending of the *Idle Man,* he endured in a state of chronic illness and despair, unable to write anything.

Dana might also have been referring to the intellectual crisis induced by his reflections on romanticism. In a fifteen-month burst of creative effort, he had explored several of romanticism's richest literary veins. He had engaged in what seemed to critics obscure experiments as he foraged for an appropriate literary genre and a coherent moral and philosophical position. In the end, his efforts seemed to come to nothing. A literary form appropriate to his talents and psychological preoccupations eluded him. The obvious appeal of transcendentalism, first considered in "Musings," foundered on his suspicion that the epiphanic moments of unity were but creations of the mind. For some romantic writers, this metaphysical crisis—this discovery that humanity is denied a privileged ground of truth—led to the recognition that the individual alone is the creator of meaning and value. It led to Emerson's assertion of the crescive, meaning-making self in his essay "Experience," to Ishmael's hard-earned but serene recognition that there is no haven on a lee shore in *Moby-Dick,* and to Thoreau's celebration of life as a continuous resurrection in *Walden.* Dana, however, could not accept a worldview that placed fatally flawed humankind at the center of the meaning-making process. He could discern few literary possibilities in the workings of the unconscious mind. The hidden processes of the mind, which for many romanticists was a rich source of symbolism, now seemed to Dana haunted by the demons of untamed passion. He took up the cause of romanticism again, but not before a Christian conversion experience in 1826 convinced him that the imagination could, after all, be reclaimed from its flawed subjectivity.

Chapter Four
Poetry's Raw Recruit

After three years of silence, Dana took up his pen again in 1825, this time to try his hand at poetry. Published in 1827 under the title *The Buccaneer and Other Poems,* his verse touched on his usual themes of nature and the psychology of the outlaw and the loner, and included as well more overtly Christian concerns about faith and the hope of redemption. In most of the poems, which were written around the time of his conversion, Dana's persona seeks consolation for the losses and disappointments of life and for the terrors of metaphysical uncertainty. In several, there is a tension between the Christian assurances he wished to affirm and the despair he felt following his wife's death and his loss of confidence in the spiritual authority of the imagination. It is apparent that he was groping for some more satisfactory way of explaining the relationship between man, nature, and God, one that gave certainty to intuition and spiritual significance to nature. His efforts are the work of a man unskilled and unpracticed in the craft of poetry. They are interesting less as art than for what they tell us about these years of confusion and doubt.

"Hauled into 'Lethe's Wharf' "

After the failure of the *Idle Man,* Dana swore to Bryant that he would not publish again, or at least not until he could afford to do so at a loss, which was "likely to come to the same thing."[1] He was often ill, complaining of nausea, headaches, difficulties with his eyesight, physical weakness, and "intellectual feebleness." So persistent were his complaints and so frequent his withdrawal from society, that contemporaries and biographers of his son, Richard Henry Dana, Jr., have suggested that he was a hypochondriac who used illness as an excuse for failure and idleness.[2] Labeling his trouble "hypochondria", however, is not helpful, because the label explains nothing while encouraging an unsympathetic view of the possibility that the circumstances of his life *made* him ill. Dana may have been reacting to the experience of being at odds with his times. If so, he was not alone.

Early European romantics who questioned the political, metaphysical, and aesthetic beliefs of the Enlightenment also were unusually prone to vague physical complaints. Marilyn Butler, in her study of the cultural context that gave rise to romanticism in England, observed that a significant number of writers complained of poor health. They were "abnormally predisposed to the kind of ailment, such as depression, hypochondria and 'nervous fever,' which was neurotic in origin."[3] She referred to Coleridge, Shelley, Kleist, Schlegel, Tieck, and Wackenroder. Like Dana, these men were not only challenging the conventional wisdom but were also fashioning the role and character of a new social type—the intellectual. Educated and self-aware yet without status or assured income, they felt isolated, rootless, and undervalued. Dana's persona Paul Felton is such a man: he has no recognized occupation but spends his time reading and brooding over large questions, his wasted talent, and a sense of social isolation. Dana was also set apart by his conservative political views. At a time when classical liberalism was triumphant in America, he was a true Burkean conservative. His illnesses may have been neurotic in origin, but if so there were many others who shared his anguished response to the place of the romantic intellectual in the nineteenth century.

He tried to find work suitable to a professional man of letters. Although he had inherited property, Dana was unable to make it yield an income and he refused to consider returning to his law practice. He heard of openings for a professor of English literature at Columbia and at a small college in Geneva, New York, but inquiries made by his friend Gulian Verplanck on his behalf came to nothing. When a position on a semiweekly newspaper published in Boston opened up, he applied without any success. He even considered writing a novel, but his heart was not in it. He confessed to Bryant that he was unable to work because of "a certain sense of heartlessness & insincerity in getting up the joy or grief of fiction—all grown out of sufferings of a terrible reality—that, had I a lion's strength, I do not know I could rouse me & shake them off."[4]

In April 1825 he was stirred from his lethargy by a letter from Bryant inviting contributions to his literary periodical, the *New York Review and Atheneum Magazine*. Dana's reviews had always been lively, controversial, and vigorously written, qualities Bryant wanted to encourage in his magazine. Bryant was a bit startled, however, when Dana's first submission was not a review but a poem, "The Dying Crow." At the age of thirty-eight, Dana felt diffident about trying a

new literary form, admitting, "I came to my work raw and ignorant."[5] Bryant was, as always, generous: "I am surprised after reading
['The Dying Crow'] to hear you say that you never wrote thirty lines
before in any measure. You have come into your poetical existence in
full strength like the first man. Not that I was surprised to find the
conceptions beautiful—that I was prepared for, as a matter of
course—but you write quite like a practiced poet."[6] Anticipating the
pitfalls awaiting the inexperienced, Dana sent all of his poems to Bryant. He urged him to "take a friendly liberty with anything I may
write—if a clumsy line, give it some of your grace; smooth a harsh
one, & bring me within poetic rules when I get out of them, which
a raw recruit is always like to do."[7]

Before printing Dana's first poem, Bryant took the "friendly liberty" of changing the title from "The Dying Crow" to "The Dying
Raven." Dana's reaction was typical of the man's stubborn independence. He wrote back: "There are some thoughts sometimes which
. . . I have an affection for, & which I should hardly be willing to
have thrust aside to humour that idle company, the public. My common Crow was magnified to a Raven upon that principle. Now tho'
there is something mighty incongruous, to my mind, in a man, in
the heart of New England, lamenting over a bird which he knows
nothing of out of Scripture."[8] Bryant offered not only suggestions,
which were largely ignored, but more important, his enthusiastic
encouragement.

In 1827 the Boston publishing house of Dearborne brought out
five hundred copies of Dana's poems. To Dana's great satisfaction,
Dearborne assumed the risks and offered him half of the profits. The
volume included eight poems, four of which had not appeared
before.[9]

The Buccaneer and Other Poems

The title poem, "The Buccaneer," is a long literary ballad about
the legendary exploits of the New England pirate Matthew Lee. The
"dark, low, brawny" Lee is a lawless, heartless, freebooter who pro-
claims, "I make the brute, not man, my law."[10] His motto is, "It is
my way." While his ship lies in a Spanish harbor for repairs, he offers
safe passage to the young widow of a Spanish nobleman slain in the
resistance against Joseph Bonapart. The pirates kill the woman's en-
tourage. Lee then breaks into her cabin, but she escapes his assault

by leaping overboard. Strange omens accompany the massacre, lending an aura of the supernatural to the events that follow. On the evening before her death, the woman appears to Lee in a dream. The ocean seems to voice a warning: "From out the silent void there comes a cry—'Vengeance is mine! Thou, murderer, too shalt die' "

Her white horse, thrown overboard by the crew, seems not to drown but to neigh menacingly throughout the night. For three years, on the anniversary of these events, a phantom ship burns in the harbor of the pirate's island refuge. A spectral horse rises out of the sea to carry Lee to an overhanging cliff. From there he reports:

> I look, where mortal man may not,—
> Down to the chambers of the deep.
> I see the dead, long, long forgot;
> I see them in their sleep.
> A dreadful power is mine, which none can know,
> Save he who leagues his soul with death and woe.[11]

Lee does not return from his third phantom ride.

"The Buccaneer" became one of Dana's most popular poems. It offered readers bold action, uplifting moral asides, and lyrical descriptions of the sea. Sensitive to both its terror and its beauty, Dana wrote several pleasingly lyrical stanzas expressing his love of the sea. The opening provides an example:

> But when the light winds lie at rest,
> And on the glassy, heaving sea,
> The black duck, with her glossy breast,
> Sits swinging silently,—
> How beautiful! no ripples break the reach
> And silvery waves go noiseless up the beach.[12]

"The Buccaneer" was more than just a swashbuckling ghost story, for it gave Dana another opportunity to depict the progressive psychological degradation caused by sin and guilt. At first Lee suppresses his fears with boasts and tyrannical acts. He then experiences the alienation from nature that is featured so prominently in much romantic literature.

> The morning air blows fresh on him;
> The waves are dancing in his sight;

The sea-birds call, and wheel, and skim.
O blessed morning light!
He doth not hear their joyous call; he sees
No beauty in the wave, nor feels the breeze.
For he's accursed from all that's good;
He ne'er must know its healing power.[13]

Finally, he sits alone upon the beach idly rolling pebbles beneath his hand, longing for the final return of the spectral horse and the "rest within the grave." This psychological portrait presented none of the distressing moral ambiguities and complexities that readers objected to in the character of Paul Felton. As the contemporary critic James McHenry remarked, the buccaneer was "a villain of real blackness" with no "sentimental admixture of good and evil." This time Dana would escape the censure of critics who expected literature to be morally uplifting. The conservative McHenry reassured his readers: "The passions and crimes of a villain, his mad career, his ruin, are a noble and moral subject of fiction in any form, and we call the delicacy that is offended by such a representation, squeamishness and bad taste."[14]

All but two of the other poems published in 1827 reflect the anguish of Dana's personal life. Dana longed for consolation. He wanted to believe that goodness and beauty lie at the heart of things, but in the teeth of so much uncertainty and disappointment, he did not know where to look for succor. Believing, on the one hand, that nature has a holy, spiritual significance and, on the other hand, that the imagination is no certain guide to these truths, Dana no longer felt confident of how the poet makes nature yield her meanings. Thus, his treatment of nature is indicative both of his uncertainty and of the growing appeal of a specifically evangelical Christian resolution to the dilemma.

The belief that a natural harmony exists linking the individual, God, and nature in one spiritual whole pervades "The Dying Raven." The poet looks on nature as an unambiguous source of emblems representing spiritual truths. The bird's presence throughout the harshest winter is a sign to the poet that there is a resurrection—spring will come. The raven is also a symbol of the spiritual richness of the natural world and commands a faith in things unseen. The poet addresses the raven as "Priest of Nature, Priest of God, to man!"

Thou spok'st of Faith (than instinct no less sure,)
Of spirits near him, though he saw them not;
Thou bad'st him ope his intellectual eye,
And see his solitude all populous. [15]

In selecting the crow/raven as his symbol of a divinity immanent
in the world, Dana ran several risks. His readers might have questioned his assigning such an august role to a bird. To this objection,
he replied with a lesson learned from Coleridge's "Ancient Mariner":

Who scoffs these sympathies,
Makes mock of the divinity within;
Nor feels he gently breathing through his soul
The universal spirit. Hear it cry,—
How does thy pride abase thee, man, vain man!
How deaden thee to universal love,
And joy of kindred with all humble things,—
God's creatures all! [16]

More seriously, his readers might have viewed this as a poetic conceit,
an association peculiar to one poet, and therefore resisted the spiritual
lesson. Dana, who had wrestled with this issue of the subjectivity of
the imagination, was eager to quash this objection. He did so by insisting that a direct correspondence exists between the spiritual laws
present in nature and the moral intuitions of humankind. The poem
concludes:

He who the lily clothes in simple glory,
He who doth hear the ravens cry for food,
Hath on our hearts, with hand invisible,
In signs mysterious, written what alone
Our hearts may read. [17]

The same assumption of a harmony between God and his creation
informs "Fragment of an Epistle." Writing to a friend to announce
his recovery from a long illness, the poet states that he has come
through his dark time because God has touched his heart with peace
and armed him with patience and with the imaginative power to
render nature in consoling and delightful ways. Shut in from winter's
"crystal bower," the poet joins, in his imagination, boys sliding
down wintery snowbanks, then "sees" the scene transformed into the

jeweled heavenly city of "Revelation." At this point in the poem, the question of the value of this imaginative play is abruptly raised. The sun, which a moment before seemed to light a path to the heavenly city of "Revelation," goes down, casting his invalid's room into gloom. The poet muses:

> Are holy thoughts but happy dreams
> Chased by despair, as starry gleams
> By clouds?—Nay, turn, and read thy mind;
> Nay, look on Nature's face, and find
> Kind, gentle graces, thoughts to raise
> The tired spirit,—hope and praise. [18]

The poem implies that the poet/narrator lays all doubts to rest by transforming the moonlit landscape into a fairy world of silvery knights equipped with fence-rail lances and sheltered by the "lovely tracery of branch and twig." In "Fragment of an Epistle," Dana's attempt to imbue objects in nature with moral sentiment is strained: the associations seem more fanciful than imagined. The more important point, however, is that he dismisses the problematical character of the imagination, which had troubled him in the years of the *Idle Man.* Instead, he suggests that nature is redemptive, or at least, that nature commands the imagination and not, as in "Paul Felton," the reverse.

Nature offers neither consolation nor inspiration in "Changes of Home." The narrator returns to the valley of his childhood, hoping to feel again the joy and delight in nature that he knew as a boy. He has lost everything—his youthful hopes, his faith in the justice of the world and the virtue of others, his beloved wife, Emmeline, and even his capacity to feel. In language strikingly similar to Coleridge's in "Dejection," Dana's narrator describes this numbing of the spirit:

> I cannot feel, though lovely all I see;
> A void is in my soul; my heart is dry;
> They touch me not,—these things of earth and sky.
> E'en grief hath left me now; my nerves are steel;
> Dim, pangless dreams my thoughts;—would I could feel!

The narrator then pleads with nature to make him whole again:

> Yet stir once more within me that pure love,
> Which went with me by fountain, hill, and grove.

Delights I ask not of ye; let me weep
Over your beauties; let your spirit sweep
Across this dull, still desert of the mind;
O, let me with you one small comfort find![19]

Nothing in "Changes of Home" suggests that nature answers his
plea. Indeed, the theme of grief and alienation is intensified by the
story told to the narrator by the village minister. Jane and Edward,
the story goes, were friends in childhood and lovers in their youth.
They are separated when Edward goes to sea in search of his fortune.
Filled with foreboding, Jane warns against the second voyage from
which Edward never returns. Like the narrator of the poem, she is
overwhelmed by grief and despair. The consolations of nature leave
her unmoved.

The conclusion of "Changes of Home" is ambiguous. Apparently
Dana meant to end the poem with a positive resolution of the narrator's dejection. Because too many memories haunt the valley of his
childhood, the narrator decides to go on his way. Before he leaves, he
states that "a sunny, gentler sense in silence stole" over his soul. On
waking he feels at peace, knowing that God's providence governs the
world. The poem ends:

No! wide and foreign lands shall be my range:
That suits the lonely soul, where all is strange.
Then, for the dashing sea, the broad, full sail!
And fare thee well, my own green, quiet Vale.[20]

The use of the word *dashing,* the reliance on monosyllables, and the
uplift of the voice all contribute a tone of hopefulness at the end. But
this resolution is undercut by associations that we could carry over
from the story of Jane and Edward. When Edward describes the sea,
he uses words of ominous portent. He refers to its "mysterious voice,"
its "maddened roar" and to "the curse that on its gloomy spirit
hung, — / 'Thou ne'er shalt sleep!' through all its chambers rung."
And it was the ocean that swallowed up the couple's dreams of happiness. So when the narrator chooses the sea over his "green vale," we
could suspect an unconscious longing for death. The poem works
against a hopeful conclusion.

"The Little Beach Bird" shares with "Changes of Home" a similar
but even more striking ambiguity. Perhaps the best of Dana's lyric
poems, it captures the characteristic sounds and movements of the

sandpiper—its "flitting form . . . ghostly dim and pale"—as it emerges from the fog, its melancholy piping cry, and "its strange accord / with the motion and the roar / Of waves that drive to shore." Like the raven, the sandpiper performs a priestly function. Its cry speaks "of a common doom." At the same time (we sense here a contradiction), it urges: "One spirit. . . . The mystery,—the Word." The terms imply a religious truth, perhaps a revelation about the kingdom of God. Dana did not elaborate.

As in "Changes of Home," he used contrasting land and sea imagery to symbolize primal moral elements. The ocean is described as a "sepulchre and pall." It endlessly sings a requiem for the dead, telling "of man's woe and fall, / His sinless glory fled." The poet invites the little beach bird, a "dweller by the sea," to flee the ocean and go with him to the safety and gladness of the green interior:

> Then turn thee, little Bird, and take thy flight
> Where the complaining sea shall sadness bring
> Thy spirit never more;
> Come, quit with me the shore,
> And on the meadows light,
> Where birds for gladness sing![21]

What is the reader to think? This last stanza suggests that bird and man can escape their fates in some fair paradise. There is no greater mystery than this Christian doctrine of redemption; but the sandpiper, which is supposed to symbolize this promise of immortality, belongs by biological law at the margins of the "complaining sea." It cannot escape. So the explicit thrust of the last stanza is undercut by the reader's recognition that flight is impossible. What remains is an uneasy feeling that life is lived at this margin between the promise of paradise and the fact of sin and death. Unexpectedly, the poem confirms another Christian mystery—man cannot elude the burden of his sinful nature.

In both "Changes of Home" and "The Little Beach Bird," the symbolic and literal meanings of the poems are at odds. Carelessness and inexperience may have contributed to this lack of integration, but it seems equally possible that the symbols reveal an unconscious level of feeling that Dana consciously meant to deny. During these three years, he seems to have been in a great muddle. He was torn between two ways of ordering his experience. On the one hand, he clung to Bryant's simple natural theology, willing himself to believe that God is present in his creation and known to man through nature and the laws engraved on the human heart. On the other hand, he was convinced that humanity is cut off from God and nature by sinfulness. Only in the poem "Daybreak" is the Christian resolution toward which Dana had been working fully realized. The theme of this poem is once again the desire for spiritual consolation. But in "Daybreak" the answer is not found in nature or in the fragile and unpredictable delights of the imagination. It arises instead from the bestowal of grace, a supernatural gift purchased by Christ's historical, redemptive act. The morning star provides the central image. Dana has the star pose a question facing all who set out to read the spiritual hieroglyphics of nature. Rebuking the weeping poet for his melancholy, the star seems to ask why nature is not sufficient for his happiness. It invites the poet to await the dawn and share in the purity, serenity, and sweetness of nature at that hour. "If thine heart be pure," the star says, put aside "the ills and pains of life," and "breathe in a kindred calm." The poet replies that nature is powerless to teach or console. At dawn nature shares his own somber mood. The gray dusky light gives neither comfort nor warmth but illuminates a "vast world [that] seems the tomb of all the dead." Although nature may have moral lessons to teach and harmonies to impart, it is helpless before man's blind greed and arrogance. The poet sees in nature only the reflections of his own downcast heart:

> It is because man useth so amiss
> Her dearest blessings, Nature seemeth sad;
> Else why should she in such fresh hour as this
> Not lift the veil, in revelation glad,
> From her fair face?—It is that man is mad!
> Then chide me not, clear Star, that I repine,
> When Nature grieves; nor deem this heart is bad. [22]

In the last two stanzas, the poet states that he has two choices: he can take comfort in the thought of death and "hopes of things unseen," or he can forsake nature, his "mother mild," and surrender to his rage and "passions fierce and wild!"

He escapes the fate of Paul Felton by an act of grace, an act that reconciles him to his life and makes nature once again radiant with spiritual significance. In an epiphanic moment, the poet's despair is swept away. Christ, symbolized by the rising sun or "crown of living fire," conquers the poet's despair:

> Suddenly that straight and glittering shaft
> Shot "thwart the earth." In crown of living fire
> Up comes the Day! As if they conscious quaffed
> The sunny flood, hill, forest, city, spire,
> Laugh in the wakening light.—Go, vain desire!
> The dusky lights are gone; go thou thy way!
> Pining discontent, like them, expire!
> Be called my chamber PEACE, when ends the day;
> And let me with the dawn, like PILGRIM, sing and pray.[23]

The allusion here to John Bunyan's *Pilgrim's Progress* seems appropriate. Dana's spiritual journey, which had begun in the faith that the writer's imagination has an affinity with the creativity of universal being, had ended in the "iron cage of despair." He now believed that the Holy Ghost must inspire the imagination and redeem nature. On the next leg of his pilgrimage, he would be accompanied by an evangelist—the Reverend Lyman Beecher.

Critical Reviews and Unfamiliar Praise

The handful of critics who reviewed *The Buccaneer and Other Poems* praised Dana's direct and economic style, command of language, and talent for describing nature. In his generally favorable review, James McHenry remarked that Dana avoided the excesses of many beginners. He did not, McHenry wrote, "mount Pegasus" to run after strange conceits or false sentiments. He also admired Dana's originality and variety of style, language, thoughts, and feelings, noting that Dana was "no harper on a tune which has been found to please the public ear—no follower of some popular poet."[24]

Bryant, who had somehow prevailed upon the editors of the *North American Review* to publish his views of Dana's work, opened with this assessment of his friend: the author, he wrote is "a man of genius, who possesses the essential qualities of a poet."[25] Bryant especially admired the integrity that drove Dana to express his feelings and ideas in his own way even when it meant inviting unpopularity. Recognizing that it was Dana's "way of attending passionately . . . to the peculiar and unhappy moods of the mind" that put readers off, Bryant insisted that there was truth and even wholesomeness in such insights. He noted similarities between Crabbe's work and Dana's "Changes of Home," but gave to the latter credit for "more fancy, more warmth, and more pathos." But it was not just Dana's strength of purpose and his ideas that moved Bryant: the nation's most respected poet found in the work of his moody friend "Teutonic strength," descriptive powers, and a forceful use of language. These critics were more flattering than Dana expected or deserved. The language of his verse was convoluted, dense, and at times obscure. He too often inverted the word order to achieve a consistent meter. Lacking a fertile imagination, he was unable to write effectively about experiences and feelings he had not had. Because his experience was narrow, Dana's poetry gives us a feeling of emotional claustrophobia.

Bryant stated that Dana had the qualities of a poet but not that his poetry fully exemplified them. Bryant believed that Dana might serve his talent better by exercising greater diligence and patience in mastering the craft. Dana had unshakable views on the subject of poetry, however, as is apparent in a marvelously revealing letter to Bryant on the subject of revising "The Buccaneer." In the letter, Dana fends off most of Bryant's efforts to bring him within the rules. When Bryant protested the phrase "thy hair pricks up," Dana replied that " 'pricks up' is the *word;* nor would any other have half the spirit." In response to Bryant's advice that he give up the colloquialism "he drowns in drink," Dana's answer was, "I cannot see that it is venturing much to venture this." When Bryant objected to Dana's reference to the inanimate ship as a ghost, Dana responded, "Now, what poetical mind ever looked upon a ship under sail (seen however clearly) other than as a *living, self-moving* creature, or hesitated about applying to it the language of his impressions?" There were many graceless lines for which Dana had an affection. He refused, beyond a certain point, to make corrections in "Changes of Home," saying, "There are things which, tho' faults in one man, in another are so connected with the character of his mind, as from their congruity with it, & making a *wholeness,* [they] lose their disagreeable effect."[26]

Although these statements appear to justify Dana's lack of self-discipline, they also reflect a considered theory of poetry. His faults arose partly from an unskillful application of romantic principles. In trying to make the language and meter of his poems correspond to the ideas and feelings expressed, Dana frequently violated neoclassical rules of poesy. In "The Buccaneer," for example, the language is harsh and the meter irregular when the action and feelings are violent; the scansion becomes regular and the language lyrical when Dana describes the beauty of the New England coastline. He also violated the neoclassical stress upon the universal experiences of mankind when he explored very personal spiritual and mental states. To his own way of thinking, his "faults" were necessary to the affirmation of the whole man.

Dana believed that despite all his faults he should be ranked among American poets just below Bryant, Longfellow, and Percival. Of course this was before Emerson, Poe, and Whitman had begun to publish. In setting himself above poets like Fitz Greene Halleck, Joseph Rodman Drake, Lydia Sigourney, and Nathaniel P. Willis, Dana was claiming no great degree of superiority! Because he was modest about his talent, it is worth considering what he may have meant by placing himself above some of his better-known contemporaries. He believed that his work anticipated a new, more spiritual and philosophical era in American literature. While others were writing satirical verse about social life in New York, religious poems recounting biblical stories, or light verse on rural scenes and domestic joys, he was exploring more complex psychological states and struggling with romantic theories of nature. Although we may see nothing particularly remarkable about his concerns, Bryant, McHenry, and others recognized the high seriousness, intelligence, and originality with which he probed spiritual and philosophical issues.

Perhaps Dana's place among early nineteenth-century American poets is best revealed by comparing him with William Cullen Bryant. Bryant was a craftsman, the first American poet to study the mechanics of versification seriously. He worked hard to perfect an easy, graceful, and accessible style, a style that would be a fitting vehicle for his optimistic and rationalistic view of the world. Repelled by mysticism or enthusiasm of any sort, Bryant cultivated, both in his life and in his poetry, moderation, good sense, and serenity. While Dana struggled for a personal response to nature, Bryant accepted without question the notion that man's moral makeup is as suited to the spiritual lessons of nature as a face is to a looking glass. While Dana wrestled with the question of the sources of the imagination, Bryant complacently assigned to the imagination the task of "infusing a moral sentiment into natural objects and bringing images of visible beauty and majesty to heighten the effect of moral sentiment."[27]

The differences between Bryant and Dana were essentially those separating the poets of the Age of Sensibility from the romantic poets. Although Bryant was certainly the better poet, and by no means one of the "five senses men" about whom Dana complained, he had

settled upon a safe, uncomplicated intellectual stance somewhere between Scottish commonsense philosophy and Coleridge's idealism.
Bryant was the best of the Fireside poets, and like his fellow poets,
Whittier, Longfellow, and Lowell, he believed that "in literature and
life doubt must issue into certitude, the original into the typical, and
the aberrant into the normal."[28] Dana could not embrace such a view
of life or of the poet's responsibilities.

The Frustrations of the Life of Letters

In addition to his poems, Dana contributed three reviews to Bryant's periodical before the niggling opposition of yet another voice of
the Boston cultural establishment prompted his withdrawal.[29] His
best review was a retrospective appreciation of the novels of Charles
Brockden Brown. Dana was one of the first American critics to recognize the importance and originality of Brown's strangely disturbing
psychological portraits. His characters, Dana wrote, "live, act, and
perish, as if they were the slaves of supernatural powers, and the victims of a vague and dreadful fatality."[30] Dana was most impressed by
the fact that the novels remained inscrutable despite Brown's efforts
to dissipate his mysteries in a profusion of rational motives and "scientific" explanations. Brown was at his best, Dana believed, when he
explored "the dusky dwelling places of superstition, death and woe"
amid scenes of "shut up houses, still, deserted streets, noisome
smells, and pestilence," as he did in *Arthur Mervyn*. Dana delighted
in characters like Carwin in *Wieland* whose deceptions were practiced
"from a hankering after something resembling the supernatural, and
an insane sort of delight in watching its strange and dreadful force
over others."[31] Although unimpressed by most of Brown's female
characters, whom he thought hopelessly sentimental and too often either indelicate or dull, Dana praised the strength of women like Con-
stantia in *Ormond* and Louisa in *Steven Calvert*. Dana also admired
Brown's gift for "making . . . characters living and breathing men,
acting in situations which are distinctly and vividly presented to our
minds."[32] Brown could do what Dana could not: he could imagine
events and characters that embodied his insights into the workings of
the human mind.

His sympathy with Brown was enhanced by his feeling that the
two were kindred spirits linked together by sharing the frustrations
of literary life in America. Both had given up careers in law to be-

come writers. Dana believed that in the absence of the support and
sympathy of friends, the decision had left Brown crippled by self-
doubts and subject to serious episodes of depression. Critics who attributed Brown's troubles (or Dana's own) to weakness of character,
Dana insisted, were men with very superficial natures. "Those who
are most apt to be tall talkers upon the duty of cheerfulness and the
danger of strong excitement," he wrote, "are mainly those, the depths
of whose feelings a fishing line might fathom, those who have no
dark, mysterious, unsounded places."[33]

Dana's enthusiasm for Brown's work did not blind him to its weaknesses. He complained of the wordy Latinate style. It reminded him
of a remark made by an English member of Parliament about Lord
Castlereagh. The member protested that Castlereagh was "airing his
vocabulary this morning." Dana also objected to Brown's rationalistic, Lockean theory of psychology. Fortunately, he commented,
Brown's insights were far more interesting and profound than the system he professed.

Soon after his review appeared, Dana had occasion to reconsider his
judgments. In a letter to his friend Mrs. Sarah Arnold he commented:

I am rather sorry that I took up so much of it with fault-finding—it was
altogether against my intentions, for he was a man of a very uncommon cast
of mind, & of a great genius. Had I written from the impression the first
reading of him made upon me several years ago, I should have been all eu-
logy. But looking at him this second time,—finding midst all his power &
genius, so much crudeness, let me say too, weakness, so much that is offensive to principle, which runs thro' his silly system of philosophizing, & all
written in the most abominable English, if English it can be called, I could
not help saying what I have said.[34]

His review illustrates Dana's talent for literary criticism. Impartial,
intelligent, and honest, he wrote critical essays based on a thorough
knowledge of English and American literature and on broad and carefully considered notions about what distinguishes good writing from
bad. Students of Brown's work today would agree in the main with
Dana's pioneering judgment of Brown's importance and failings.

Just as Dana was beginning to enjoy literary work again, he was
caught up in the snares of the old feud that had destroyed his career
as a critic for the *North American Review*. In 1826 the *New York Review
and Atheneum Magazine* was merged with the *United States Literary Gazette* of Boston to form the *United States Review and Literary Gazette.*

From that point on Dana had to conduct his business not with Bryant but with the Boston editor, Charles Folsom. Folsom was an instructor of Italian and a librarian at Harvard, a Unitarian, and a scholar. In Dana's view he was also humorless, timid, and pedantic. A member of the literary and social club formed by William Prescott, Folsom was not sympathetic with Dana's romantic ideas. The two clashed head-on over the publication of an essay written by Dana's cousin, Walter Channing. Channing's essay, "What Is Nature?" was hardly revolutionary. His views on Locke, education, and nature were those that had been urged by Coleridge, Wordsworth, Bryant, and Dana for years. Nevertheless, Folsom complained that "there was much in [the essay] to make one stare." He agreed to publish it reluctantly and then only because Dana had revised the piece and had insisted that Bryant would admire it. Folsom promptly wrote Bryant and complained of Dana's opinion that "a style, which I know not how better to designate than as Wordsworthian . . . ought to displace the prevailing manner of writing in our Journals. On this subject," he added, "there was formerly a controversy among the conductors of the N. A. Review, as you probably know."[35] Bryant took a conciliatory tack, agreeing with Folsom that Channing's essay was obscure but insisting that such metaphysical speculation was rare in America, where a "worldly material spirit" prevailed. The inclusion of such material, Bryant advised, would "agreeably diversify the pages of our journal."[36] Folsom was unconvinced and unreconciled. He rejected Channing's next contribution, an essay on the Boston Atheneum, and demanded revision of Dana's review of Anne Radcliffe's Gothic novel *Gaston de Blondville*. Dana wrote to Bryant bursting with indignation over this interference. "I would gladly write for you at odd times . . . could I feel at perfect liberty. . . . But I can't work in freedom. Folsom is a 'gentleman,' &, I am told, an accurate scholar; but he is too timid, or too formal, or too something. He objected very childishly, I tho't, to some things in the article now in press. Not caring much about it, I altered.—I can't however, write under such restraint.[37] The *Review* was too "grave," he wrote, and could use some of his own "head-over-heels folly."

One of the sentences to which Folsom objected poked fun at the shallowness of Unitarian ideas about morality. Folsom, however, left in a more subversive jibe at Scottish commonsense philosophy. Rumor had it that Radcliffe, in good Lockean fashion, had gotten the necessary firsthand sensory experience of "hauntedness" by staying a night in the fine old Gothic mansion of Haddon House. But Dana had discovered, to his great delight, that the story was untrue. In all probability, he wrote, she had spent the night in some dull, ordinary bedchamber in Litchfield. In case the reader missed his point, he added that the imagination does not need the stimulation provided by such research: "There are powers in some minds, let a certain chord be touched in nature, and to what sweet and universal harmony do they wake! . . . They need no musician to instruct them—the teacher is within. Look into your Locke, or your [Dugald] Stewart, and explain it if you can."[38] Dana made the changes required by Folsom. He even went on to write his review of Brown's novels. In truth he really did not care. He chafed at the "armloads" of silly, worthless books sent him to review and was far more interested in writing poetry.

Dana was heartened by the early sales returns on *The Buccaneer.* He looked forward to bringing out a second edition. Within six months, however, interest in the little volume of poems had faded. Not even the strong reviews by Bryant and McHenry could bolster the declining sales. By June 1828 he was again without prospects. Half jokingly he told Bryant, "I am ready any day of the week to hang myself because of having nothing else to do."[39]

Chapter Five
Dana's Christian Romanticism

When a revival movement swept through Boston and Cambridge in the winter of 1826, Dana was left in its wake, a penitent at the mourner's bench. Descended from a family that had traditionally been associated with the Congregational church, he had sympathized for years with its more liberal tendencies. He had looked less to religion, however, than to the "poetic imagination" for answers to spiritual and philosophical questions. The anguish and uncertainties that had accompanied his devotion to the Coleridgean theory of the imagination were eased by his conversion experience. For the next decade, Dana gave himself up to the religious controversies of his day, carving out a place for himself among Christian romantics.[1] During these years he also forged a new philosophical and aesthetic point of view, combining elements of his earlier romanticism with the precepts of evangelical Christianity. He believed that in Christianity he had discovered a higher ground for the romantic vision. In the three reviews written during these years, he proved himself to be a shrewd observer of the religious and cultural tensions dividing the orthodox Congregationalists, the Unitarians, and the Transcendentalists. Although Dana's poetry was at times argument dressed out in meter, his satire in "Factitious Life" is genuinely amusing and the lyricism of "Thoughts on the Soul" reveals that his "rough voiced muse" was acquiring fluency and melody.

Battling the Unitarians

The great religious revival that had been boiling away in New England for more than a decade did not reach Boston until 1826. In that heartland of Unitarianism, orthodox Calvinism was still, as Harriet Beecher Stowe remarked, "the despised and persecuted form of the faith. It was the dethroned royal family wandering like a permitted mendicant in the city where once it had held court."[2] The Unitarians dominated the ranks of the wealthy, educated, and genteel, controlling the courts, the press, and Harvard University. In the hope of rekindling the old faith, the leaders of the languishing Hanover Street Congregational Church of Boston sent for Reverend Lyman Beecher.

Beecher was as tough and pragmatic as the proverbial Yankee peddler. He had the rustic's manner of speech and a "cut and thrust" style of preaching that broke "all Boston rules of pulpit etiquette."[3] He watched his listeners, he studied their faces for signs of distress and conviction, and then "struck just according to character and case." In the winter of 1826, Beecher took his campaign to Cambridge, where he preached on the themes of "A Change of Heart" and "Regeneration." He warned his listeners about the moral desolation that would surely sweep the land if they accepted the teachings of William Ellery Channing, whose recent sermon on "Man's Likeness to God" had stunned the orthodox.[4] Dana was there when Beecher set the "dry bones shaking" in Cambridge. Illness, bereavement, feelings of failure, and spiritual confusion made Dana sensitive to Beecher's tactics.

Moreover, Beecher's sermons played upon the fears and nostalgia that Dana shared with many whose lives had been dislocated by the early phases of the Industrial Revolution. Beecher railed against the wealthy merchants, lawyers, and politicians, whom he held responsible for economic and social upheaval and against the Unitarians, whose influence, he believed, contributed to a decline in morality and religious piety. Dana, who lacked both wealth and the status accorded to those in recognized professions, had felt humiliated when his family was supplanted from the circles of power by the "raw gentry." For years he had smoldered with indignation about the influence that a small Unitarian elite exerted over cultural affairs.

Neither Beecher nor Dana approved of those who wielded power, so they placed their trust in plain men who did not. It was not that they believed in equality; they simply had no other partners in the quarrel with the dominant groups in their society. Beecher tried to mobilize democratic hopes for essentially conservative ends. Although he dreamed of establishing a hierarchical social order ruled by the regenerate, he appealed to every individual's aspiration for equality and full participation. Similarly, Dana, when the *Idle Man* fared badly at the hands of professional critics, claimed that original poetry and fiction were best understood by "sensible, self-taught men, who live out of what we choose to call literary society, and who have been in the habit of trusting to their own understandings."[5] Evangelicalism and romanticism sprang from similar impulses. The evangelical minister, like the romantic poet, distrusted rational discourse, favoring instead emotional appeals to the majesty of God and the mysteries of the heart. Those with common enemies make good, if temporary, allies. So it was that Dana, who by birth if not by wealth, might have been numbered among Boston's "blues," found himself leagued with the rustic Beecher in a campaign to reestablish orthodoxy in Boston.

Although these social, political, and cultural issues were important, the impetus behind Dana's conversion was chiefly spiritual. The shaft in the evangelist's quiver that penetrated all of his defenses was the charge of intellectual pride. Beecher accused his listeners of relying upon their understanding rather than upon revelation and the grace of God. In retrospect Dana considered himself as guilty as anyone of "substituting a vague sentimentality, and beautiful, floating, and no less vague thoughts of some ideal, in the place of the revealed God."[6] He wrote to his son Richard Henry, Jr., that he was "humbled & mortified at the recollection of [his] former contempt for evangelical views."[7] For a time, Dana became obsessed with the spiritual complacency encouraged by Christian liberalism and with trivial sins of dress and deportment. His literary reviews and correspondence were drenched in self-abasement. Convinced that most people have no concept of the awfulness of sin, he wrote tedious, self-righteous letters to his sons and friends pleading with them to repent. He scolded his good (and patient) friend Sarah Arnold for wearing her hair in curls and for "getting a little too much . . . into what men are pleased to call the world."[8] To Richard Henry, Jr., and Edmund, Dana reported a news story about a young college man who had been crushed to death when his loaded cart overturned on him. The letter concluded with the chilling advice: "Be ye also ready."[9]

Some years later, when Richard, Jr., came across letters written to him by his father before his conversion, he commented to his wife: "They show how we lived, acted, felt before the demon of Calvinism and Revivalism got hold upon the family. It looks as though we might have been trained up a cheerful, kindly affectioned, religious household, with our pleasures and friends about us. But the flower of our youth from twelve to twenty was under a cloud. The clouds had rolled off, and we were getting into light and warmth again after we moved to Boston [1835]; but the effect of those years on us all . . .

never can be quite erased."[10] Although the younger Dana had no real understanding of the complex reasons for his father's guilt and despondency, he correctly sensed how completely the "demon" of Calvinism saturated their lives for nearly a decade.

Dana's first skirmish with militant Unitarians occurred right after his conversion. The conflict absorbed his time, contributed to family discord, and deepened his mistrust of Unitarianism. Beecher's revival brought to a head a long-simmering feud between the orthodox Congregationalists and the Unitarians of Cambridge. The minister of the First Congregational Church of Cambridge, Abiel Holmes, was a mild but determined Calvinist who, at the height of the revival, decided to discontinue the practice of exchanging pulpits with ministers holding more liberal views. The Unitarians, who constituted a minority among church members but a majority in the parish, protested Holmes's action. Appealing to a Massachusetts Supreme Court decision (1820) which ruled that for legal purposes the parish was the church, the Unitarians demanded that Holmes resume the exchanges or face dismissal. Holmes refused, declaring: "If I seem to disregard the wishes or the tastes of my hearers, it is because I am more desirous to *save* than to please them."[11] The Unitarians then voted to bring the issue before an ecclesiastical council.

Dana, along with five others, made up the church committee responsible for preparing the case for the orthodox. Dana and the committee sought to win for the church the right to an equal voice in the selection of ministers to sit on the ecclesiastical council. Had they succeeded, the rights of the church in any dispute between the church and the parish would have been recognized and the threat that the more numerous Unitarians posed would have been lessened. But they lost. The council was made up entirely of Unitarians who ruled that Holmes's religious beliefs were pernicious and opposed to reason, rectitude, and piety. Outraged by the high-handedness of the proceedings and by the Unitarians' claim to having all reason and truth on their side, Dana decided to write a detailed account of the controversy for posterity. The dispute led him to examine the views of the Unitarians with an acute and discerning eye.

The dispute also colored relationships within his own family. Dana's elder brother Francis, who had led a wandering, mercantile life after his disastrous youthful speculations, acted as a leading spokesman for the Unitarian side. Dana believed that had it not been for Francis, he might have pursued his literary career free from the

oppressive burden of financial insecurity. Now their relationship was
further strained by religious conflict. What may have given this family rift a special pathos was Richard Henry, Jr.'s, apparent admiration
for his scapegrace uncle. Describing Francis's influence among the
Unitarians of Cambridge, Richard, Jr., remarked that his uncle was
a man with "great personal beauty, a commanding & graceful figure,
beautiful voice, dignified manners" and admittedly, an irritable
temper.[12]

For a time, Dana's literary efforts were closely related to the religious controversies of the day. He contributed three reviews to the
Spirit of the Pilgrims, a periodical established by Congregationalist
leaders to counter the Unitarian religious press.[13] During this same
period, he wrote two long religious poems, "Thoughts on the Soul,"
which he read before the students of Andover College in 1830, and
"Factitious Life." Although both the essays and poems reflect his orthodox beliefs, they do not deal specifically with doctrinal issues.
Dana's conversion did not divert him from the questions raised by his
romantic concerns but gave him instead a new framework within
which to view them.

His most perceptive analysis of the religious culture of his day appeared in a review, printed in 1830, of Isaac Taylor's *Natural History
of Enthusiasm.* In this essay he predicted that a new spiritual philosophy would arise from an inevitable backlash against the cold, rationalistic system of the Unitarians. His criticism was unlike any other to
come out of the orthodox camp. In substance and spirit, it resembled
judgments made a few years later by transcendentalists—the dissident
Unitarians who led the way to this new spiritualism. Dana would
never join the transcendentalists: he thought them little better than
atheists. Still, he knew he was a brother in spirit who shared with
them many romantic ideas about man, nature, and the imagination.

Dana looked upon Unitarianism as an episode revealing the dynamics at work in humanity's timeless struggle to achieve a balance between faith and reason. He began his essay by arguing that, from a
psychological point of view, the individual requires a religion answering to both the material and the spiritual sides of his nature. The
individual yearns, Dana argued, to comprehend the "Infinite Unseen"
in its spiritual essence while, at the same time, demanding some tangible evidence, some proof to the senses, of God manifest in his creation. Dana believed that the history of the past revealed a cyclical
alternation between periods that gratified one or the other of man's

psycho–religious needs. In the eighteenth century, people entered the materialist phase of the cycle. Viewing their growing mastery of nature as proof of the power of reason, they dismissed religious belief as childish superstition. They defined God to suit the requirements of reason, "employed [him] to wind up the machinery of the universe," and regarded the divine mysteries as "an insult and an offence." The void left by this materialism, Dana insisted, generated a longing for things of the spirit and a counterimpulse toward pantheism. Poets began to discover God in the beauty of nature and the souls of men.

Unitarianism was born in the eighteenth century and, according to Dana, contained within it these very same tensions. Unitarians were "practical materialists" who, in Dana's opinion, offered too little nourishment for the human spirit. In the process of reconciling faith with science, they had sacrificed the spiritual content of Christianity. When some biblical doctrine seemed at odds with natural reason, the Unitarians discarded it. They denied that their God was simply another name for natural law; but what sort of God is it, Dana asked, that can be understood so exclusively in human terms? Too proud to accept the limits of human knowledge, the practical materialists, according to Dana, "refuse to contemplate God, except in his infinitude. . . . Our God is made an abstraction, and our hearts grow cold, and the heavens void."[14] Out of bits of philosophy, poetry, and ethics, the Unitarians had made a perfectly rational religion. Nor could it be otherwise, he wrote, for their religion is the product of human reason alone. They worship themselves: "The man becomes a pleased and constant worshipper; and well he may, for his God is the issue of his own brain, and from out himself he worships himself. Behold the progeny of human pride,—the Creator the creature! the creature the Creator![15]

Dana believed that a new "spiritualism" would emerge out of the void left by this arid, overly intellectualized view of God. At first people would be tempted into a "religious sentimentality," seeking comfort in an idealized spiritual presence, a "sort of atmospheric divinity [that] breathes around us like a balmy day, and, like a Claude sky and light, wraps heaven and earth in soft transparency."[16] When their minds inevitably wearied of such an abstraction, they would then turn to nature. Like primitive people who fashioned idols out of wood and stone or like the eighteenth-century pantheists, these disaffected Unitarians, exhausted by a "continual efflux through infinitude after such an abstraction," would fall down and worship nature.[17] A few years later when the Unitarians became embroiled in a controversy over Emerson's "Divinity School Address," Dana looked on with both alarm and the intellectual satisfaction of knowing that he had foreseen it. He would have been a less perceptive critic had he not also been tempted by the idea that God reveals himself through nature. Only his doubts about the imagination—his suspicion that the imagination reveals the poet's inner self rather than any higher reality—had kept his own "spiritualism" in check.

In a long satirical poem, "Factitious Life," (1832), Dana exposed the folly that he believed resulted from the influence of rationalism, and especially Scottish commonsense philosophy, on the manners and morals of the Unitarians. From his first public utterance, he had criticized materialism, conformity, and the unqualified belief in reason and progress. He had created heroes who had railed and suffered, but neither he nor they seemed to have a clear target for all this rage. Now he believed that he had found his target and could explain what had gone wrong in Boston. In substituting commonsense philosophy and Unitarianism for idealism and religion of the heart, the people of Boston had sold their souls for a mess of pottage.

In "Factitious Life" the speaker recalls a time when "Great Nature" was man's teacher. People trusted their own hearts and were moved to joy, sorrow, and indignation by a natural flow of feeling. But times had changed. Under the influence of Scottish philosophy, the feelings essential to a generous heart and a just society had become suspect. Even courtship was blighted. The speaker comments:

> . . . should you beg a maid her ear incline
> To your true love, she bids you love define;
> Then talks of Dugald Stewart and of Brown,
> And with philosophy quite puts you down;
> On mood synthetical, analysis,
> Descants awhile.—Most metaphysic Miss!
> Who'd win thee, must not like a lover look,
> But grave philosopher, and woo by book.[18]

The speaker complains that to talk of sin or to plead against injustice is thought to be in bad taste; to give way to passion is thought imprudent if not vulgar. Briskly and effectively he condemns the moral cowardice induced by the tyranny of public opinion:

With etiquette for virtue, heart subdued,
The right betraying, lest you should be rude,
Excusing wrong, lest you be thought precise,
In morals easy, and in manners nice;
To keep in with the world your only end,
And with the world, to censure or defend,
To bend to it each passion, thought, desire,
With it genteelly cold, or all on fire,
What have you left to call your own, I pray?
You ask, What says the world, and that obey.[19]

In Dana's view, such an emphasis upon gentility and common sense could only get in the way of an impassioned, perhaps mystical, encounter with God.

His purpose in writing this poem and his review of Taylor's *Natural History of Enthusiasm* was not merely to expose the contradictions and folly of Unitarianism. He was more interested in demonstrating the superiority of orthodox Christianity. Having shown that the Unitarians had failed—the materialists because they "lord[ed] it over the material world, as if no God created and sustained it," and the spiritualists because they looked "through all spiritual existences and relations, as if no revelation were needed . . . to behold them"—he set out to prove that orthodox Chrisitianity satisfied people's spiritual and philosophical needs.[20] Unlike most contributors to the *Spirit of the Pilgrims,* Dana did not build his case on analysis and biblical citations. Instead he integrated Christian doctrines with his earlier romantic ideas and preoccupations. In the doctrine of original sin, he found an explanation of the individual's alienation from God and nature. Out of the spiritual crisis caused by conversion, he believed that an individual acquired powers of insight that otherwise lay dormant. In his review of Taylor's book, he observed that in conscience-stricken man "the workings of the soul wax stronger and stronger, and he sees into himself with a power of vision almost . . . supernatural,—not to philosophize about himself, not even, it may be, with a purpose to know himself [though self-knowledge is the result]. . . . When man shall form his philosophy, not by wandering to the ends of the earth after his God and to become acquainted with himself, [as Locke and the commonsense philosophers believed] but shall learn that the Life and Light come from God's Spirit, and must be within himself, or cannot be to him at all," then true philosophy is his.[21] Finally, in the Christian doctrine of redemption, Dana believed he had found the solution to the metaphysical uncertainties posed by the subjectivity of the imagination. A deepened understanding of Platonism provided him with a strategy for integrating Christianity and romanticism. Since his youth, Dana had been familiar with the poetry of the seventeenth-century Cambridge Platonists. His reading of Coleridge's extended commentary on the work of Platonists Henry More and Archbishop Leighton in *Aids to Reflection* suggested to him a way of reclaiming the awesome powers of the imagination.[22] Platonists believed that God had given order to the cosmos by projecting his ideas into material form. Dana expressed this notion in his poem "Factitious Life": "The earth but shows / What, ere in outward forms they first arose, / Lived spiritual, fair forms in God's own mind."[23]

Through the faculty of the imagination, humans share in God's creative power. They cannot trust this power absolutely, however, because they are imperfect; their humanity separates them from God and from fully participating in the divine fecundity. In the opening stanza of his "Thoughts on the Soul," Dana describes in unmistakably Platonist terms, the soul's creative powers and the consequences of man's otherness:

> It is the Soul's prerogative, its fate,
> To shape the outward to its own estate.
> If right itself, then, all around is well;
> If wrong, it makes of all without a hell.[24]

Later in the same poem, he tells again of the fate of all his tormented heroes:

> Who has no inward beauty, none perceives,
> Though all around is beautiful . . . .
> He makes a turmoil of a quiet world;
> And fiends of his own bosom people air
> With kindred fiends, that hunt him to despair.[25]

Before his conversion, Dana's ideas about the spiritual significance of nature had been confused and ambiguous. He had recognized that nature is powerless to heal the Paul Feltons of the world. But he had also believed that because God is immanent in his creation, the contemplation of nature can open the way to spiritual truth. Christian Platonism made it possible for Dana to overcome this difficulty.

By 1830 he was convinced that the Holy Spirit, which redeems the soul at the time of conversion, also takes possession of the imagination, enabling one to see the spiritual meaning of nature. In "Factitious Life" Dana dramatized the contrast between the poetic act of infusing nature with moral associations and the spiritual vision opened up to the redeemed person. After toying with some of the more conventional associations (flowers teach humility, mountains nobility), the poet abruptly rejects such spiritualizing of nature and sets before the reader a new vision of nature made possible by salvation:

> . . . behold
> The earth unveiled to thee, the heavens unrolled!
> On thy transformed soul celestial light
> Bursts; and the earth, transfigured, on thy sight
> Breaks, a new sphere! Ay, stand in glad amaze
> While all its figures, opening on thy gaze,
> Unfold new meanings. Thou shalt understand
> Its mystic hierograph, thy God's own hand.

If the difference between meditative daisy-picking and a confrontation with God in all his creative vitality was not yet clear, Dana drove the point home in the next stanza.

> "From nature up to nature's God," no more [shall man]
> Grope out his way through parts, nor place before
> The Former, the thing formed: Man yet shall learn
> The outward by the inward to discern,—
> The inward by the Spirit.[26]

The subjectivity of the imagination need hold no terrors for the redeemed poet.

"Factitious Life" celebrates the self-reliance born of reliance on God. Dana seemed to feel that self-doubts spring from experiencing the world dualistically. When the individual feels himself set apart from the community, when the truths of the heart seem opposed to the truths of reason, when the imagination seems torn between private subconscious visions and nobler universal ones, when the things of the sensory world seem to corrupt spiritual concerns, then there can be no certainty, no rest for the soul. For Dana the great beauty of Christian Platonism was that it cut the ground from under this sort of dualism. Because God is present in the soul of the redeemed individual and because God is also present in all material forms in the world, there can only be one universal undivided reality. Life in "the One" ends all self-doubts. Dana describes the redeemed individual:

> Now all is thine; nor need'st thou longer fear
> To take thy share in all. The far, the near
> To thee, are God's,—so, thine; and all things live
> To higher ends than earth; and thou dost give
> That life which God gives thee; and to impart
> Is to receive; and o'er thy new-born heart
> The earth and heavens pour out a living flood;
> And thou, as God at first, seest all is good.[27]

Dana thought Channing and Emerson's notions about man's likeness to God the purest egotism. Yet his own ideas about the power and prerogatives of the redeemed poet were much like theirs about the individual attuned to his or her spiritual nature. Dana was upset by Channing's claim that notions of God are derived from examining the human soul. He was no less alarmed by Emerson's assertion that in the simple and spontaneous obedience to our higher instincts, "we become divine."[28] But he did not disagree with their views of the individual's aspirations and possibilities. He differed only in believing that these possibilities must be quickened by an act of divine grace.

Seeking a More Spiritual Religion

The orthodox Congregationalists could not take much comfort from Dana's attacks on the manners, morals, and beliefs of the genteel Unitarians, for they too became the targets of his criticism. He had originally turned to evangelical Congregationalism because the imagination could not satisfy his longing for an immediate experience of "the One." Dana soon realized, however, that the kind of mystical experience he described in "Thoughts on the Soul" and "Factitious Life" was not really trusted by the evangelicals. He was an idealist while they, like the Unitarians, were students of Scottish realism. He sought union with a transcendent spiritual reality while they sought a balance between the religion of the heart and the counsel of reason. The romantic impulses that had driven him into Congregationalism were left unsatisfied. His love of beauty flew in the face of a Calvinistic asceticism, and his mysticism went beyond the bounds of common sense. Dana could not be kept for long within sectarian traces. He found that a temporizing, Arminian spirit was taking hold among some of the orthodox.[29] In his review of *Natural History of Enthusiasm,* he argued that Scottish commonsense philosophy was corrupting Congregationalists as well as Unitarians. Nathaniel William Taylor, an associate of Beecher's and a professor of theology at Yale, took pride in demonstrating that orthodox theology conformed in all respects to the principles of reason and common sense. Thinking it vital to adapt to the optimism and democratic temper of the age, both Taylor and Beecher emphasized the importance of free will. They believed that too much stress on the traditional doctrine of man's wretchedness and dependency would impede the conversion experience by discouraging moral effort. Dana, who deeply felt man's utter dependence on God, was convinced that the evangelicals' emphasis on heartfelt religion merely masked their shallow rationalism. He chided them for acting out of the fear that they might be thought less enlightened than their opponents. They seem to think, he wrote, that the Bible, without their efforts, will "turn out at last not wise and philosophical enough for advancing reason."[30]

Aesthetic concerns played a surprisingly important part in Dana's growing disillusionment with the Beecherites. When, in 1828, he was asked by the Reverend Enoch Pond, editor of the *Spirit of the Pilgrim,* to review Robert Pollock's poem "The Course of Time," Dana placed his romantic principles above his sectarian loyalties. Pollock's admirers believed that only John Milton had written a better religious poem; but Dana thought it preposterous that readers regarded orthodoxy of opinion sufficient grounds for praising a poem that was monotonous and long-winded. He decided to give readers a lesson in romantic aesthetics.

In true Coleridgean fashion, he likened the imaginative powers of the poet to those of God at the time of creation. The poet, he wrote, must have a temperament in which "all coming from him is first fused, and then, running into the mould of the imagination, is turned out a true form. . . . The thought must appear to have arisen out of the depths of the soul; out of those depths all things must have come up, whether man, or beast, or creeping thing; yea, regions fairer than earth must rise out of them, as rose the earth above the waters, self-moved, effortless, and instinct with life."[31] It is a mark

of his renewed confidence in the imagination that Dana could savor
with such enthusiasm its unconscious sources.

A poet is not great, he told Pollock's admirers, just because he
holds orthodox opinions and writes in verse. He must above all else
be inspired: "There must be the life-giving, the forming, and the in-
forming principle: though the mind thinks, it must be from a feeling
as if it were from some mysterious impulse communicated to it from
the soul deep within; otherwise, though all may be wise and good,
and in tolerable verse, it will not have in it the great and distinctive
qualities of poetry."[32] Pond knew that readers would not like to see
one of their favorite poets so summarily dismissed. Before publishing
the review, he invited the Reverend Joseph Emerson to write a letter
to the periodical challenging Dana's criticism. When Dana heard
about this, he accused Pond of unsound journalistic practices. He
added that if he and Beecher wanted more agreeable opinions they
had better find themselves another man.[33]

Dana was also repelled by the spiritual pride, prudery, and excessive self-denial of many Christians. He felt that the sort of person
who praised bad poetry because it supported orthodox dogma was
likely to campaign, as Beecher did, against wine, Sunday steamboat
excursions, and other innocent pleasures. Although sometimes guilty
himself of such scrupulousness, Dana came to recognize its dangers.
In a review of Henry Martyn's *Memoirs,* he complained of the sort of
sour-stomached Christians who dwelt on their troubles and spiritual
anguish to the exclusion of the joys and serenity imparted by religion.

Dana's intimacy with the painter Washington Allston encouraged
him to take this more positive view of pleasure. Their friendship,
which had begun in the days of the old Monthly Anthology Society,
had grown over the years, especially after Allston's marriage to Dana's
sister Martha in 1830. They had undergone similar life experiences:
both had begun their careers as ardent admirers of Coleridge and
Wordsworth and both had experienced a traumatic loss of confidence
in the imagination.[34] By 1830 each had staged a strategic retreat into
Christian romanticism. After years of philosophizing together, their
aesthetic ideas were quite similar. Like Dana, Allston buttressed his
faith in the imagination by invoking divine inspiration. In his post-
humously published *Lectures On Art,* Allston referred to the "abiding
Interpreter" who "holds in subjection the last high gift of the Creator, that imaginative faculty whereby his exalted Creature, made in
his image, might mould at will, from his most marvellous world, yet

unborn forms of beauty, grandeur, and majesty, having all of truth but his own divine prerogative,—the mystery of Life."[35]

For Dana, as for many other Americans including Irving and Hawthorne, Allston was the epitome of the artist. Allston's sweetness of temper, elegant manners, and orthodox religious views cast a reassuring aura around his mildly hedonistic way of life. Richard Henry, Jr., recalled in his journal the delights of evenings spent in Allston's company—the cigar smoke "aetherial[izing] the whole," the "social glass of wine," and the parlour fire that inspired a meditative mood.[36]

Dana came to share Allston's conviction that God had annexed a sense of pleasure to the exercise of the individual's moral and intellectual faculties. In his review chastizing priggish Christians, Dana told readers that God created the universe as one harmonious whole. The beauties of nature were intended to draw people away from their dark introspections. As Dana explained: "External beauty awakens in the healthful mind a pleased internal sense of the beautiful; and as, by its own law, the mind seeks to produce what is within, it becomes generative of the beautiful, and, as it does so, more perfectly realizes its own idea and what is without."[37] He believed that the senses are given to administer to the soul. If we truly know and love God, he argued, this love will sanctify our pleasures. He warned the censorious and ascetic: "Let us not, then attempt to be wiser than God, or think that he has been mistakenly indulgent in bestowing upon us so many faculties for intellectual culture and bodily enjoyment."[38] It was a comment inspired by the evenings at Allston's. Dana offered these criticisms with some misgiving, for he did not want the "sensuous" Unitarians to draw the wrong conclusions. He knew how impossible it is to show "that the renewed in heart have endured unnecessary self-infliction, without its being made an occasion to question the depravity of man, and the whole plan of grace and salvation growing out of that awful truth."[39] Still, he felt the risk worth running for the sake of a more joyful Christianity.

Having parted company with the New Haven theology of Taylor and Beecher, Dana was once again looking for a spiritual home. For a time he was attracted to the variety of Calvinist theology taught at Andover Seminary. He was friends with Leonard Woods, Sr., a professor of theology at Andover and a defender of Calvinism in controversies with Unitarians. Dana and Woods were both suspicious of the Arminian influence at Yale and Harvard and shared similar views of man's depravity and dependence on grace. When Richard Henry, Jr., was suspended from Harvard in 1832 for his minor part in a scrape with college authorities, Dana entrusted him to the moral and intellectual guidance of Leonard Woods, Jr., a tutor at Andover. Although Andover was, from Dana's point of view, doctrinally correct, it was not intellectually exciting. The most interesting statements of Christian Romanticism were being made by European theologians and philosophers who had had no influence on Andover's faculty.

A handful of Americans were, however, beginning to urge these ideas, as Dana noted in an enthusiastic letter to Bryant in 1833: "There are a *few* truly great minds coming up on the horizon; tho' they do not rise quite so fast upon us as the natural sun, yet they are rising. These minds are mostly turned to philosophy; but it is a spiritual & poetical philosophy, &, therefore, the only true. . . . There must be a good deal of error along with this, for some time, but it will pass off. Religion in all its spirituality is to be seen & felt pervading nature & the arts."[40]

At about this same time, he began corresponding with two American champions of Christian Romanticism, James Marsh of the University of Vermont and Caleb Sprague Henry of New York University.[41] Both men devoted their lives to developing philosophical grounds for belief in orthodox religion. Like Dana they felt that the influence of Lockean psychology among Protestant sects in America was generating absurdities and preparing the way for skepticism. Marsh, who admired romantic writers, especially Byron, Madame de Staël, the Schlegels, and Herder, had published an American edition of Coleridge's *Aids to Reflection* in the belief that it reconciled the doctrines of the gospel with the subjective foundation of the faith. The foundation to which Marsh referred was "Reason," Coleridge's term for the spiritual principle in man that intuitively perceives truths above sensory experience.

Caleb Sprague Henry's views were similar to Marsh's. A graduate of Andover and a convert to Episcopalianism, Henry was responsible for publishing American editions of the work of Victor Cousin, a French philosopher and critic of Locke and British empiricism. Though neither Marsh nor Henry could be called a great mind, both must have seemed so to Dana, who had lived most of his adult life without experiencing genuine intellectual and spiritual companionship. To know others who to some extent shared his beliefs must indeed have seemed like the dawn of a new era.

Dana's correspondence with Marsh and Henry ranged widely over the many issues that leagued them together against the Arminians on the one hand and the transcendentalists on the other. He and Marsh discussed Taylor's rationalism, Emerson's "Epicurean Atheism," and the pantheistic tendencies of the younger Unitarians.[42] Dana certainly agreed with Marsh's assessment of the problems and needs of the age: "We need within a deeper, & more heartfelt, & heart protecting, practical piety, or else a more vigorous & profound philosophical spirit. . . . We ought to have both, but how are we to obtain them?"[43] With Henry, who was interested in the political and social implications of Christian romanticism, he discussed the dangerous influence of English writer Thomas Carlyle, whom Dana called the "very Ego of Egotism!—the *I* Myself, I," and those equally troublesome "Jacobins" of Boston—Orestes Brownson, George Bancroft, and George Ripley. Dana kept his friends informed about the progress of the transcendentalists and tried to enlist their help in combating the friends of the "Democratic Principle."[44]

Dana's spiritual pilgrimage ended in 1843 when he was confirmed at Saint Paul's Episcopal Church in Boston. He expressed his approval of Episcopalianism as early as 1835, three years before his son Richard and daughter Charlotte were confirmed in the church. He feared at first that the ritual was a substitute for faith and love, but he was soon won over. In 1844 he was one of the founders and senior warden of the Church of the Advent, the first church in America to embrace the Anglo-Catholic movement. This movement called for a return to the liturgy, spiritual discipline, and ritual of the Anglican church before the influence of the Puritans. At the Church of the Advent, services were held daily, Holy Communion was celebrated every Sunday, the Psalter was chanted, and the priest, Rector William Croswell, wore the surplice and knelt before the high altar.

The attractions of High Church Episcopalianism for Dana are not hard to imagine. It appealed to his love of "old times," traditional architecture, and music. As historian Sydney Ahlstrom has noted, the Anglo-Catholic movement heralded a revival "of philosophical idealism which brought with it a recrudescence of mysticism and Platonic thought as well as an interest in metaphysics."[45] Thus, Episcopalianism offered Dana an alternative to Congregationalism and transcendentalism. Equally important, Dana's membership was consistent with his political views. As his dissatisfaction with democracy grew, he clung to institutions that, through traditions and forms, visibly embodied the hierarchical principle that he believed should govern society.

Critical Recognition

Evidence of a growing interest in "spiritual and poetical philosophy," and especially the enthusiastic response of students at Andover to "Thoughts on the Soul," prompted Dana to bring out a collected edition of his work in 1833. The publishers, Russell, Odione & Co., agreed to print one thousand copies of his poems and the *Idle Man* stories. He was paid a hundred dollars for the copyright, a sum that finally offset his losses from the *Idle Man* venture. After a lifetime of writing, Dana had not yet profited a single cent.

At first the critical response was discouraging. Once again the editor of the *North American Review* refused to publish a review of Dana's work. Complaining of the illegibility of the manuscript submitted, Alexander Everett returned it to the author only to refuse it again in clean copy. The review published by the Unitarian periodical, the *Christian Register,* so carefully balanced the merits and faults of his work that Dana felt he had been praised only to give an appearance of fairness to the faultfinding. The reviewer noted Dana's originality but found him wanting in "everything that belongs to the style of poetry." Although he admired the purity of Dana's moral and religious feelings, he added that he did not agree with the theology that inspired them. He suggested that Dana's prose style could be explained only on the assumption that as a boy he had had a negligent professor of rhetoric.[46] Dana felt, and with some justification, that if he had been a Unitarian he would have been treated more generously.[47] "How few friends—how many enemies have I!?" he groaned.[48]

Just as Dana was about to sink into the depths of self-pity, the foremost Unitarian periodical, the *Christian Examiner,* printed an enthusiastic review by C. C. Felton. Felton made it clear that, in his view, Dana was an important writer, the author of "some of the most remarkable works that our country has ever produced."[49] Using imagery drawn after the New England landscape, Felton aptly described the contrasting tones in Dana's writing. "They are full of power, but of a dark and gigantic character, enlivened here and there by the softest traits, like sun-lit and verdant openings among bare and rugged and desolate hills."[50] He admired Dana's sometimes masterful use of language and his terse, individual style, a style that "reaches farther into our most hidden and mysterious emotions; it takes a stronger, a more *fearful* hold on our minds, than the style of any other author within our knowledge. Thoughts of the most tremendous import are crowded into a paragraph, a sentence, a line, nay, a single word."[51] Felton singled out "Changes of Home" and "Domestic Life" for particular praise because they were morally instructive and spiritually uplifting.

Dana was touchingly pleased by Felton's complimentary remarks. He was so unaccustomed to praise that he did not seem to notice how deeply Felton objected to much that was central to his outlook. Like most Unitarian moralists, Felton thought that literature should depict the universal in human experience not the exceptional, the compliance with social conventions not the defiance of them. He would grant neither the artistic legitimacy nor the truthfulness of Dana's psychological portraits. He wrote of the story "Paul Felton":

> We do not think such works come within the legitimate scope of creative art. They leave on the mind an impression of unmixed, unmitigated gloom. They do not represent man as he is, scarcely as he can be. They seem like the wanton play of a most powerful imagination, carrying out a monomania, with torturing ingenuity, into all its possible conditions, into all conceivable terrors, through all the most loathsome details of raving madness, compared with which a Bedlam is the very Temple of Reason.[52]

Dana's conviction that men of sensibility and moral grandeur find life in America almost intolerable, also offended Felton, who complained: "He describes man, not as he is, nor as he appears in the *ideal man* of other poets and of artists, but according to peculiar conceptions of his own. There is not a single character among his heroes, who is at peace with himself, able to curb his spirit, and do battle against outward circumstance, with his mind in vigorous action, his heart aright, and his body whole."[53] It was true, of course, and yet it was the sort of judgment that had less to do with the merits of Dana's work than with the importance attached to conformity and gentility by the class Felton represented.

Henry Wadsworth Longfellow's hearty, generous review appeared in the *American Monthly Review*. Admitting that he had no head for metaphysics and no interest in Coleridge, Longfellow expressed impa-

tience with the more speculative of Dana's poems. He pointed out
that too often Dana's verse occupied some halfway ground between
prose and poetry. As for the merits of the controversial "Paul Felton,"
Longfellow asserted that while not for those of "pure and quiet
mind," the story exerted a "fearful power over the soul" of those
whose terrors and passions were at all like Felton's. Despite his reser-
vations, Longfellow admired Dana and understood his importance.
On encountering Dana's work for the first time, Longfellow wrote,
one immediately felt oneself "in the presence of a highly gifted intellect," interested not, as were most of his contemporaries, in light and
sentimental musings, but in the serious work of reflection and writing. "As a poetical thinker," Longfellow continued, "Mr. Dana has
no superior,—hardly an equal in the country; as a mere versifier, we
could point out several who are his superiors."[54] This distinction between thinker and versifier is a highly useful one. Though not a first-
class writer, Dana was a precursor of great ones. In an age when most
American writers were content to imitate the English, beat the drums
of patriotism, and give voice to the shallow homilies of the Unitarian
Enlightenment, Dana was thinking his way through some of the aesthetic and metaphysical questions of concern to the next generation.

The most perceptive discussion of Dana's fiction appeared in a review by the Reverend Nehemiah Adams, pastor of the Essex Street
Church of Boston. His essay was published in the *Literary and Theological Review*, a periodical conducted by Dana's friend, the younger
Leonard Woods. Adams likened Dana to the discoverers of unknown
continents. Dana's psychological portraits, Adams wrote, explore partially known truths about the human mind and soul and illuminate
the "awful recesses" of our original nature. He especially admired the
characterization of Paul Felton who, he assured readers, suffered the
fate of many who are driven into the "dangerous profound" by a misdirected longing for the infinite. Adams attributed Dana's psychological insights to his personal afflictions and thoughtfulness, and to his
Calvinistic belief in sin and spiritual redemption.

Adams overestimated the part played in Dana's fiction by Calvinism. At the time he wrote "Paul Felton," Dana was not a Beecher
convert but was struggling instead with a private psychological hell
created by his recognition of the unconscious sources of the imagination. Dana made it hard for any critic to identify these romantic influences in the story by inserting in the 1833 edition a new
paragraph. The paragraph attributes to Felton religious ideas that

Dana had not formulated until the early 1830s. In the original passage, Felton explains to his father-in-law the unity of soul and sense that he experiences in the presence of nature. The 1833 version, however, reads like a summary of ideas set out in Dana's review of *Natural History of Enthusiasm*. He has Felton express distaste for the notion of God as "a sort of universal intelligence" while affirming a belief that we can only overcome the radical difference between our sinful, finite nature and God's infinite holiness through the person of Christ.[55] In the light of this addition, it is not surprising that Adams and later critics believed that the tale was about the ravages of sin and guilt.

Although wrong about the sources of Dana's psychological insight, Adams was right to stress its originality and importance. To modern readers, the characters of Paul Felton and Tom Thornton seem melodramatically wrought and their motivations obscure and peculiar. But in the early nineteenth century, when the conventional view of human nature was dominated by the superficially optimistic notions of the Scottish philosophers, Dana's stories went some way towards recognizing psychological complexity. Readers who objected to his work, Adams argued, either willfully ignored the existence of such complexities or lived their lives "on the surface of their souls." Their carping made him think of a "fire-fly venturing into a cloud, and rebuking the eccentric lightening and the restless thunder."[56]

Even the critics who admired Dana's work did not know quite how to place him among his contemporaries. They recognized his originality without quite understanding its origins and character. Their own religious and philosophical loyalties inevitably colored their reactions, but Dana was grateful for any recognition at all. He confessed to Bryant: "The kind feeling toward me wh' these late instances have shown, have touched me even to sadness; as *praise* I have hardly thought of it, it has gone so straight to my heart."[57] There was more to come. At last he received the much coveted recognition of British reviewers. Reviewers for the influential *Blackwood's* and the *Edinburgh Review* gave Dana's poetry a full measure of praise and criticism.

Dana was in his midforties when he received these modest signs of public recognition. As he looked back over his small collection of stories, poems, and critical essays, Dana might truly have said that he had been faithful to his calling as a man of letters and to his own personal vision. He had begun his adventure of the mind as a youthful admirer of the late eighteenth-century English poets. Inspired by Coleridge's ideas about the creative imagination, he had moved from the positive romanticism of "Musings" to the despairing, negative romanticism of "Paul Felton." He had obeyed the romantic injunction to trust the visions of the imagination only to discover that the quest for the inwardness of experience led not to transcendent truths but more deeply into the unconscious mind. His conversion and rediscovery of Platonism had brought his intellectual pilgrimage out onto sunlit, level terrain. A Platonized Christianity seemed to promise not only salvation but also a redemption of the imagination. He felt assured of possessing the truth above sense, a truth that did not raise the risks of madness, atheism, or solipsism.

It had been a remarkable journey, one that Dana had taken alone. Coleridge would have understood it: Poe and Melville would later, and each in his own way, experience some of the same metaphysical and spiritual dilemmas. But of Dana's contemporaries, perhaps only Allston had any notion of these issues. The transcendentalist Amos Bronson Alcott, who was a shrewd observer of his contemporaries, correctly estimated the toll that Dana's isolation had taken: "He was an early admirer of a higher order of poetic genius; and early gave to the American public, his regard for the great names of Coleridge and of Wordsworth.—With encouragement his career would doubtless have been more brilliant; and his mind have done better justice to its powers." As an afterthought Alcott added: "I cannot but think his theology is, in part, at fault."[58] Dana, however, would have protested that his religion had saved him from the romantic nightmare of a world that is no more than a projection of the self.

Chapter Six
Critic of American Culture

In the 1830s, lectures became a major source of public entertainment. The country was in a millenarian mood, eager to hear about America's glorious prospects and tirelessly receptive to the theme of "the spirit of the age." Pressed by financial hardship, Dana resorted to the lecture circuit, speaking on topics ranging from Shakespeare to women's rights. Whatever his subject, his overriding concern was the mediocrity of American culture. Others might speak of the nation's material and political greatness, but Dana demanded that his audiences consider why America was so uncongenial to her writers. Perhaps he was drawn to this question by the need to understand his own failure and feelings of alienation. Certainly his own frustrations gave him genuine, if sometimes harsh and self-serving, insights into the more oppressive dynamics of the national culture. He warned his listeners that several of the values they most prized—equality and freedom from the burdens of the past—were also the ones most responsible for this mediocrity.

His vision for America was so conservative that it seemed revolutionary. He urged a return to the values of simplicity and spirituality, and lamented the passing of hierarchical institutions. He attacked majoritarianism as tyrannical and suggested that the individualism of Americans was an illusion. The communitarians of the period were hardly more utopian or hostile to the dawning age of industrialism and mass culture than Dana. All of his life he had wasted himself in unyielding opposition. Nevertheless, his perspective enabled him to write some of the shrewder and more discerning cultural criticism of his day.

Dancing in Chains

How Dana had managed to support himself and his family during twenty unsuccessful years as a writer is something of a mystery. He probably lived on a small rental income from inherited land along the

Charles River. By the mid-1830s his financial situation had become desperate. A realistic appraisal of his finances in 1834, accompanied by bitter reflections on his brother's old speculative losses, sent him to bed with a bilious attack and a fever. With Richard enrolled at Harvard's Dane Law School and Ned at the University of Vermont, his circumstances had become "straitened in the extreme."[1] In spite of some favorable reviews of the 1833 edition of his works, Dana knew better than to expect to make money from his writing. So, to avoid starvation, he turned to teaching and lecturing, the last resorts of the impoverished man of letters.

He first considered teaching in the fall of 1834 when Charles Follen told him of plans to create a "literary institution or college in Boston." Follen, who previously held a temporary professorship of German at Harvard, had been fired for expressing strong antislavery opinions. He invited Dana to accept the post of instructor in English literature and composition, explaining that "no one that I know in this country is more competent than you to fill" it.[2] Racked by self-doubts, Dana secretly wished that the project would fail. He wrote to his daughter Charlotte, "I am almost afraid of its success, such doubts have I of my fitness for the work."[3] He was relieved to learn that there were not sufficient funds to establish the school.

In 1835, when financial stress got the better of his anxieties, he organized a class in English literature for women in the Boston area. His project was promoted by his cousins William Ellery and Edward Channing and by George B. Emerson, an educational leader and proprietor of a private school for young women. The classes, which he taught for three winters, met for one and a half hours two times a week in his home at 10 Sutton Place. The tuition was ten dollars. Some of Boston's wealthiest citizens—the Lawrences, Jacksons, Crowninshields, Sturgises, Storys, Channings, Websters, and Welleses—enrolled their daughters.

Although his teaching methods were progressive, Dana must have created a rather somber atmosphere in the classroom. He rarely lectured but relied instead on conversation, hoping that this informality would encourage a freer exchange of ideas. He was unfailingly kind and courteous for he shared the gallant attitudes toward the "weaker sex" that were characteristic of his age and class. Some students were overawed by him, some were intimidated by having to speak in front of the others, and his experiment in informality seems to have been only partially successful. He wanted, above all else, to "fix" in his students a lifelong love of literature; but his moral earnestness had a way of tempering enthusiasm. He explained to Mrs. Arnold that he wished to immunize them against "life's frivolities;—to let them see that Lit. is not a *thing* bound up in calf & morocco, but a manifestation of their own inner being;—to open principles, not detail facts."[4] If his purposes were a bit somber, he nonetheless brought to his task a thorough knowledge and love of his subject and an originality of mind.

He found teaching neither profitable nor congenial. In his first year he probably earned around $1000; in his third and last year, only $250. It was the work itself, however, that made Dana feel like a man in chains. He was put off by having to explain to his students how a piece of literature worked. "I don't like the work of dissecting, even if it be to put the same together again," he told Bryant. "I feel as if it were irreverential; & the sense of reverence for something out of my own soul is necessary to my soul's life."[5] Dana also resented having to prepare for class when unmoved by spontaneous delight. He was most troubled by the conviction that teaching was taking him away from his real work, draining him of the energy, inspiration, and time needed to write. Leonard Woods, Jr., editor of the *Literary and Theological Review,* and Caleb Sprague Henry, editor of the *New York Review,* both urged him to submit anything he might write—poetry, reviews, or essays. Nevertheless, Dana declined for he felt that teaching made creative work impossible. As he explained to Mrs. Arnold:

> I do long to be free, that I may work my mind according to its bent. For a few years past the desire has been working strongly in me to get hold of a fitting subject for a poem of some compass, & to devote to it, if need be, the remainder of my life. But I can't dance in chains—there have been men strong eno' to do so—I can't write poetry while my heart is heavy & my spirit anxious about outward means to outward ends. . . . I will not complain, altho' I sh'd be much obliged to some of the abolitionists of the day, if, in the plentitude of their benevolence, they w'd find out a way to set me free; for I am infinitely more a slave than the Sambos & Pompeys for whom they are turning the world over & over.

Recognizing that his metaphor had lured him into mawkish self-pity, he added, "Don't think fr' this that I hold to slavery."[6] Of course he did complain! And he probably deceived himself in thinking that, under easier circumstances, he would have been a significantly better

writer. He might have been a more productive one, however, for it
is certainly true that he allowed his poverty and lowered status to prey
upon his mind and damage his health.

Dana found a partial answer to his financial troubles in the growing
popularity of public lectures. In the 1830s the lecture platform became an important force for adult education and social reform. Writers, who might make very little from their published works, could
earn enough to get by on in a season of lecturing. In 1833 he gave
his first public lecture on "The Past and The Present" before a Lyceum audience. Two years later he delivered the Independence Day
oration in Salem, Massachusetts. By 1838 he had worked up a set of
eight lectures on literature and Shakespeare, which he repeated many
times over the next twelve years before audiences throughout the
northeastern and central United States. After making his last lecture
tour in 1850, he calculated that he had earned a net profit of roughly
$4611 in fees. He had also earned a reputation as an authority on
Shakespeare. Despite the hardships of traveling in winter and the
added stress on his health, he rarely complained of these lecture tours.
The occasional small audience discouraged him, but on the whole he
seems to have enjoyed the travel, the social contacts, and the role of
a literary celebrity. Although Dana mistrusted the motives both for
seeking and for granting public fame and had always gloried in the
role of outsider, he longed to be taken in, petted, and approved of.
He might make slighting remarks about the "blue-stockings" and the
"big bugs," but he felt especially gratified when the leading citizens
of a community came to hear him.

American Culture and the Alienation of the Writer

In several of the lectures that Dana gave in the 1830s, he attempted to explain why American culture had such a paralyzing effect
upon literary talent. Over the years he had often written about the
experience of alienation. Although he knew precisely what he disliked
about American society, he had never gotten much below the surface
of things. His analysis had been obscured by the romantic belief that
genius can rise above circumstances, by the notion that his disappointments were due to his own personal demons and private failings,
and by the hope that a good revival would put it all right. By the mid-
1830s, however, Dana had shaped his inchoate feelings of isolation
and despair into a theory of cultural criticism. American writers, he

claimed, were as gifted with imagination and power as their English counterparts. They were lesser writers, "not from the native poverty of the poetic mind of this age, but from the comparative meagreness of society."[7] No writer, not even one of great genius, could, in his view, "unfold independently of his surrounding society." Like many other American writers in the nineteenth century—Cooper, Irving, Longfellow, Hawthorne, and later, Henry James—Dana felt that this meagerness was due to the absence of traditions and the dull sameness of social life.

His criticism of American culture started from the premise that the writer, like God, creates out of an overflowing of love. God's creativity is a necessary manifestation of his nature, but the writer can create only when he finds in his experience objects that answer to his love. The writer must, Dana argued, find beauty in nature and warmth and sympathy in those around him, or else the love that fuels the imagination will waste away. "We must be in sympathy with our world," Dana wrote.[8] If the world proves unlovely and unpoetic, the writer escapes by turning in upon himself. Dana believed that in America the writer cannot help being alienated. To act the part expected of him by society, the writer must repress the ideas and feelings that are most essential to him as a writer. The true self is at war with the social self. In one of his most autobiographical comments, Dana described the alienation of the poet of his day: "As his sympathies are contracted, or cut off, the poet, in his poetic character, grows unsocial; and when he would mingle with men, it must be upon the condition of suppressing his deeper impulses and more imaginative state. The consequence is, that the poet-man—and the man-poet—the entire man—cannot mingle with the world. He does but lend to it for the time his outer, inferior self;—the inner, superior self is kept back in its secret abiding-places—for it cannot be satisfied where it most craves to be."[9] Cut off from the relationships with people and nature that contribute to a sense of the spiritual unity of all things, the poet experiences an intolerable loneliness.

Dana believed that writers were evolving two ways of dealing with the unpoetic quality of contemporary society, neither of which was satisfactory. One led into the unconscious mind and madness, the other to a lifeless and ponderous metaphysics. Poets cut off from their society, Dana wrote, may become obsessed with their own states of mind, especially with the working of their imaginations. They may even become convinced that their own psychological states are the

only source of poetic truths and that creativity is not possible without
alienation. This "solitary and unhealthy confinement of the spirit,"
Dana remarked, encourages morbid thoughts, dries up diversity, and
yields writing that is suffused with a "certain egotism."[10] He pointed
to Byron as an example of such an obsessive, morbid poet, and Poe
also fitted the description, but, of course, Dana's best example was
himself. Indeed, his portrait of the egotist was a self-portrait, dated
1821.

The second path led to a style of writing that was more philosophy
than poetry. Dana believed that as people have fewer opportunities to
experience the harmony between nature and themselves, the poets
who want to represent this harmony find themselves drawn to metaphysics. Because nature has been both tamed and ravaged, the images
and associations that once arose spontaneously must now be produced
by metaphysical thought. The poet overreacts to the skepticism of the
age: "Not content with letting the spiritual influences of nature glide
silently into him, he must needs be profound and metaphysical upon
them, and philosophise the plant and man, the one out of its materi-
ality, the other out of his humanity, into little else than abstrac-
tions."[11] With method so much in evidence, the naturalness and
spontaneity of poetry are lost. Dana thought that Wordsworth's poetry exemplified these philosophical excesses. Anxious to demonstrate
the value of poetry to an unbelieving age, Wordsworth too often reminded his readers that in poetry about nature "there is a deep philosophy."[12]

Dana's diagnosis of the dilemma facing the modern poet was perceptive. He understood that being a poet in an unpoetic society, and
especially in America, called for extraordinary measures. He knew
well that the subjectivity of the possible strategies—the egotism of
the one and the metaphysical idealism of the other—made the dilemma that much more difficult in a society that placed such a high
value upon common sense and the world of everyday experience. The
problem was not insoluble, however. As critic Roy Harvey Pearce has
shown, Emerson and Whitman worked out strategies whereby a primary egotism could achieve universality through the language of poetry.[13] Dana did not: he had tried, of course, but his resort to the
Holy Spirit of the evangelists would hardly satisfy an increasingly sec-
ular nation. If Dana did not come up with a solution, he had gone
farther than any of his generation toward identifying the problem. In
his middle age, he had to be content with explaining why America

was so antipoetic. He offered two fundamental reasons: the first, the ignorance of Americans about the importance of the past; the second, their passion for equality.

There can be no poetry, no genuine culture, Dana argued, when the mind of a people is so wholly confined to the present. In his essay "The Past and The Present," he drew an analogy between the plight of a nation that denies the importance of the past and the plight of an individual who is aware only of immediate sensory experience.[14] In Dana's opinion, an individual governed only by the senses would have no genuine awareness of a self. The mind would be like a "pudding stone," an "aggregation of unchanged, foreign bodies, adhering . . . not so much by any elective affinities as by some external propulsion."[15] He was convinced that a sense of self is the result of an organic process, an ongoing awareness of a personal, unique past. Similarly, a nation acquired an identity through the collective consciousness of its history. A nation without a strong sense of its history, he believed, is like an individual without a sense of self—both are imbecilic.

Of all people, Dana wrote, Americans are the least philosophical. By cutting themselves off from the past, they make their world unintelligible. Americans act as though someone had drawn the small circle of the present around them and required them to explain everything in terms of what lay solely within the circle. Under such circumstances, Dana asked, how is a knowledge of cause and effect possible? How is one to discover the relationships among things or to recognize the spiritual origin and the unity of all things?[16] Because of this ahistorical, circumscribed view, he argued, Americans think of the state as a "great piece of machinery," and of the citizen as a small, indistinguishable bit in the whole. Bound to the state by utility rather than by ties that lie buried in tradition, Americans feel alone and rootless. They become easy prey to the many pressures to conform. "Going forth without a strong individuality of character," which develops only from a sense of the past, "men assimilate carelessly and unconsciously with the circumstances, views, and notions which happen to be in fashion at the time. A conventional uniformity gathers over the multitude; manners take the place of character; and how to bear one's self, and how to express one's self, and not how to think and feel, become the object of life."[17]

The moral consequences of this present mindedness worried Dana as much as the social and political ones. Because Americans evaluate matters solely in terms of the interests and needs of the present generation, decisions are made without any perspective. In the absence of traditional rules and obligations, the people prefer the "respectable" to the "permanent principle of perfectness and truth."[18]

What ultimately saps a culture of its vitality and robs poets of their calling is the conviction, if widely held in a society, that no meaning exists beyond the surface of things. Indifference to the past, according to Dana, has a crude, materializing influence on American culture. It is, in Wordsworth's terms, the "retrospective virtues" that are most responsible for spiritual wisdom and poetry. The powers of association, the creative imagination that ascribes to objects their spiritual and symbolic meanings, the capacity to commune with the ideas that have inspired humanity since ancient times, all arise from intercourse with the past. Dana was convinced that an exclusive concern with the present threatened to blind Americans to their highest end. He warned his readers:

> Living in the present alone, the imagination is bounded by the visible and actual, its combinations are lessened in number, and its creative power held in check, and it can no longer go out into the invisible, no longer expand and exalt itself by the loftier and purer excellences of the ideal, or call into being creations around which the affections may gather, and be made indeed alive with conceptions and emotions, speaking of a higher original, and prophesying a return up thither, through infinite love. Thus it is that the soul is kept unconscious of its finer powers, and loses even its longing after something better and nobler than any thing that *is*.[19]

Without the imagination, there can be no knowlege of God nor any grasp of the mysterious relationships and affinities that link the spiritual and material realms.

The Cultural Impact of Egalitarianism

In "Law as Suited to Man," Dana argued that the principle of equality and the values and customs to which it gives rise, exerted a damaging influence on American culture. The essay was originally delivered as a Fourth of July oration in Salem, Massachusetts, in 1834. Those who heard the speech hardly knew what to make of it. There probably was not a speaker in the entire country that day who was so willing to challenge America's most cherished beliefs. Some years later Edmund Quincy recalled the impact of Dana's speech:

A few years ago the good people of Salem invited him to deliver a Fourth of July oration, and what does he select for his subject but the necessity of an hereditary monarchy and a house of peers to a well-ordered state! He at least deserved the credit of having selected a new topic on a day when all the old ones had been worn to rags. His audience were [*sic*] aghast, and there was some talk of tar and feathers or of riding him out of town upon a rail, but on the whole they concluded to leave him to the stings of his own conscience.[20]

There is something typical, even bleakly inspiring, about Dana's determination to speak of the dangers of equality before an audience gathered to celebrate the signing of the Declaration of Independence. Although Quincy was probably correct about the implications of the speech, he was mistaken in thinking of it as primarily a political statement. The speech floated airily above the surface of Democratic and Whig party combat. Dana did not discuss the political issues of the day: there was no mention of the Bank of the United States, the Cherokee removal, or President Jackson's preemptory method of leadership. There was no discussion of such issues as property rights, consitutionalism, or the role of government in the economy. He was not trying to promote partisan goals but rather to define, from a conservative philosophical vantage point, the basic principles at work in American culture.

Dana chose a timely topic because the future of democracy was very much on the minds of both Americans and Europeans. Like adolescents before mirrors, Americans from George Bancroft and James Fenimore Cooper to Dana's friends Gulian Verplanck and C. S. Henry scrutinized the national profile for flaws and beauties. In 1831 the brilliant French aristocrat Alexis de Tocqueville visited America hoping to discover for his countrymen something about their democratic destiny. His *La Democratie* or *Democracy in America* was published in Paris in 1835 and in Boston in 1841—too late to have exercised any influence on Dana. Had Dana's remarks been merely an Anglophile's defense of monarchy and hereditary classes, they would be interesting only as queer artifacts. But like Tocqueville, Dana set out to chart the impact of equality on American culture. And, like Tocqueville, he believed that egalitarianism was largely responsible for the tyranny exercised by the majority, the restless quest for wealth, and the mediocrity of American literary and intellectual life. This is not to suggest that Dana's speech rivals Tocqueville's work. One would be hard put, however, to think of a work by any other American in the 1830s that so shrewdly analyzed the cultural consequences of the American passion for equality.

Dana prepared the way for his critique of democracy by arguing that individual freedom can exist only in a hierarchically organized society. By freedom, Dana did not mean, as did most of his contemporaries, either the absence of constraints or the condition secured by constitutional guarantees. He reached back into the seventeenth century, perhaps to the work of theologian Richard Hooker, for his definition of freedom. He argued that freedom is the power to live in obedience to the will of God. Like his Puritan ancestors, he insisted that institutions exist to ensure this obedience. To the perennial question, after what model should such institutions be designed, Dana replied with ideas borrowed from the Platonists.

It is humanity's task to replicate on earth the divine pattern apparent in the creation. He believed that God had ordered paradise and created all things in nature in hierarchical patterns, rank above rank, to ensure a perfect harmony. Because there can be no contradictions in God's plan, because a correspondence exists between things of heaven and earth, "the rule of this world must be after the pattern of the heavenly, . . . teaching, in the main, the same lessons, and acting upon the same attributes of man."[21] Institutions organized by ranks manifest in tangible forms the divine principles of obedience and order. It follows, Dana reasoned, that people who live in a democratic society where God's will is obstructed by egalitarian social forms cannot be truly free. They cannot obey God's will because their institutions do not embody his divine order.

In his opening remarks in defense of a hierarchical social order, Dana sounded very much like John Winthrop aboard the *Arabella*. When, at one point in his oration, Dana invoked "the prophetic fears of our Fathers," he was not referring to the patriots' dread of English tyranny but to the Puritans' fear of popular and feeble forms of government. Though he insisted upon the similarities between his views and those of the Puritans, there was this difference: when forced to choose between the needs and interests of the individual and those of the colony, Winthrop (the Puritan) decided in favor of the latter. Dana, on the other hand, although he valued community, judged the success of social institutions by their impact on the individual. Romanticism had carried him further from his Puritan roots than he realized, for what mattered to him was the ability of the society to nurture autonomy, self-realization, and authentic individuality.

He told his Salem audience that the desire for equality destroyed spiritual values by encouraging discontent and an insatiable search for wealth. In hierarchical societies, he said, there is a security of place and possessions. Differences among classes are clearly marked by accent, manners, clothing, and a variety of privileges. Each individual knows his or her place, and if it is less exalted than that of many others, it is nevertheless endeared to the individual by traditions and familial associations. The security afforded by hereditary classes ensures contentment. But in America serenity and respect for authority, he claimed, are constantly losing ground before the trampling feet of ambition. No one is content. Everywhere there is a restless, all-pervading, all-absorbing love of gain. Because absolute equality is as yet unrealized, and probably unattainable, the demand for change becomes insatiable. No institution is allowed to stand undisturbed lest it perpetuate unwanted distinctions or mask some as yet unconquered vestige of usurping authority.[22]

In traditional societies, Dana said, the ethical principles of subordination and respect for authority are enforced by the institutions of monarchy, nobility, and the established church. Over the centuries, people learned to accept the implied limitations on their will as lawful and necessary. In democracies, however, individual egotism is unbounded. No institution exists that can stand as a rebuke to pride and self will. Discontent and infidelity thrive where the correspondence between the divine and mundane order has been broken. Although our religion teaches humility, he remarked in a letter to Mrs. Arnold, the politicians cry, "We are all sovereigns," and every "wraprascal in the nation [is encouraged to say to his president] 'I set you up there to serve me!' "[23] He was, of course, more cautious in his comments to his Salem audience—there were no references to wraprascals—and yet, his ideas must have struck his listeners as quixotic if not downright un-American. Most of his countrymen would have found discontent a small price to pay for the material rewards of ambition; and a certain disregard for authority was, in their eyes, better than the loss of the rights of self-government.

Like Tocqueville, Dana was struck by the fundamental paradox generated by Americans' simultaneous commitment to freedom and equality. In his oration, Dana posed the paradox in these words: "In our Form of Liberty, then, is there not a subtle and pervading spirit of bondage weighing upon the freedom of the soul of man?"[24] In his view, both politics and culture in general suffered as a result of the unrestricted power of the majority. We are a people, he remarked, who pride ourselves on being the freest in the world, but in truth we are the subjects of a pervasive tyranny. The will of the majority is absolute. In hierarchically organized societies, power is not exercised by one authority alone but is broken up by ranks, modified by a variety of privileges and responsibilities, and held in check by institutions that are a part of the establishment but go beyond political authority. In an egalitarian democracy, however, there are no such constraints: the will of the people, expressed in law, is pure force. What gives the majority its awesome power is the fact that the people feel their psychic identity only when acting in their capacity as the majority. No common origins, no shared sense of the past, no traditions unite them into one people. Only when acting as the majority do Americans satisfy a deep longing to participate in a collective identity, and for this reason, the majority "brooks no opposition."[25] It is hardly surprising that the people of Salem were outraged. He told them that they were little better than slaves at a time when most Americans prided themselves on their individuality. He pointed to the irony in the fact that a people who began "with setting up the Rights of Man and arraying self-will against established Law, [had] come round to making the individual but an instrument of the political mass, absorbing his will into what is called the Will of the People, . . . so that while he is absolute as a mere portion of this mass, in his individual capacity he is left without a right."[26] The individual cannot resist the will of the majority, Dana said, and is left "a lonely spirit [standing] on his lonely plain."[27]

Dana believed that the tyranny of the majority, while offensive in its political guise, was even worse in its tendency to supress cultural diversity. In societies organized by rank, he argued, the individual is encouraged in his or her distinctiveness. Traditions tend to preserve variety, families protect their eccentrics, and social ranking encourages differences among and within the various orders. But in a democratic society, everyone is ground down into a drab, conventional sameness. The love of equality is responsible for "that tyranny of opinion, which leaves to no man the freedom of his own thoughts; that prying spirit, which *mouses him out* in his most secret retirements; and that meddling disposition, which puts shackles upon the freedom of his words and acts."[28] The schools provide institutional support to these homogenizing influences. In the name of equality, all children are treated alike regardless of differences in talent, circumstances, and inclinations. In the end, the uniqueness that belongs to each child is lost. By preparing everyone for a future that only a few will attain, the schools, he argued, "fill the head with vain fancies, and destroy simplicity of character," while teaching "little of real knowledge, and less of true wisdom."²⁹ The churches also promote conformity for they too have embraced democracy and so no longer teach the spiritual virtues of humility, gratitude, contentment, and empathy.

Many of his politically conservative contemporaries believed that the demand for equality also posed a threat to private property. When workers or "agrarians" spoke of equality, conservatives feared an end to inheritances or a redistribution of wealth. Dana argued that such a loss of property would be of small importance when compared with the way egalitarianism diminished the value of spiritual and intellectual excellence. The spirit of equality, he wrote, "deprive[s] each individual of the free exercise of his moral endowment and intellectual powers . . . for it takes away the motive to their exercise, and thus destroys their life in robbing him of their rewards."³⁰ It was, he believed, a form of oppression without precedent.

Soon after publishing a revised version of his oration, Dana wrote to Mrs. Arnold acknowledging how old fashioned his views were:

There was certainly some mistake about the time of my birth—I'm an impersonated Anachronism. Interiorly I'm a gothic Cathedral, or a baronial Castle entertaining nobles, knights & ladies, minstrels, menials, gypsies, ghosts, & familiar faries [*sic*]; on my towers astrologers outwatch the Greater or the Lesser Bear, & forecast the noble lovers' fate, or the destinies of nations. I look out, & all around me I see my oaks felled, my deep forests opened to the day, & cross-cut turnpikes, canals & railroads;—nothing left of what belonged to that within, nothing to wed sympathy with, nothing like what *once was*—unless it be that madly driving, fire & smoke monster—(wh' some one called Hell-harnessed). . . . Am I not an anachronism then?³¹

He was indeed an anachronism, but his essay was not quite so daft as Edmund Quincy's or his own remarks might suggest. It is unlikely that he believed any hierarchical society, let alone that in England, actually worked the way he described. His traditional society, like the "baronial Castle" in his letter, was an imaginary place—what modern sociologists would call an ideal type. Like his other all-encompassing category, "old times," it served him as a base against which to compare his own society. His comments to Mrs. Arnold suggest that the social and political philosophy described in his essays was inspired by his regrets over the loss "of what belonged to that within." In other words, it was the mediocrity of American culture and its unfriendliness to the writer that made hierarchical societies and old times so attractive.

Some, Dana admitted, will think this cultural poverty small reason for objecting to egalitarian democracy or the passion for progress. But, he insisted, "there is nothing more serious than poetry." Poetry is a "manifestation of the dearest faculties and affections of man, in their greatest strength, beauty, and variety."[32] A society uncongenial to poetry is unfavorable to human nature; a society that alienates its poets is a society built on false principles.

In his orations, Dana had transformed years of brooding alienation into an interesting and perceptive contribution to the debate on the national culture. Never impressed by the earlier arguments that attributed the mediocrity of American letters to a dependence on England, or to materialism and practicality, he had tracked the problem into the heart of the American consciousness. In a few years Emerson, Thoreau, Hawthorne, and others would take up some of the themes that Dana discussed in these essays. Some writers were, at that moment, working out strategies for making America the subject of great literature. This new generation of writers would share some of Dana's misgivings about democracy, but none would so totally renounce their own national culture.

Lectures on Shakespeare

Dana gave his first set of lectures on Shakespeare in Providence, Rhode Island, in 1838. On Tuesday evenings from mid-October to mid-December, he delivered eight lectures, receiving what was for him the gratifying sum of $521. Shakespeare's popularity in America almost guaranteed Dana an audience. By the late 1830s, the plays, which had been thoroughly absorbed into the nation's popular culture, were being enjoyed by people of all classes throughout the country. Numerous editions of Shakespeare's complete works had been issued in America, and journals had been offering appreciative historical accounts of him since about 1810.

Despite this interest, no American critic of any stature had yet appeared. Dana's lectures were the first instance of romantic Shakespearean criticism in America. His interpretations of *Hamlet* and *Macbeth* are particularly remarkable. Both bear the unmistakable signs of his Christian romanticism and are intelligent and original approaches to the plays. Dana did not go before his audiences primarily to instruct them in Shakespeare, however. His object was to shake them from their complacency, jar them free from neoclassicial literary values and priggishness, and convince them that no nation could aspire to greatness if it did not place supreme value upon the arts. He loved Shakespeare and the Elizabethan Age, but like his "old times" and "baronial Castles," these topics served as points of comparison against which to measure his country's cultural shortcomings.

Dana mistrusted public lectures and approached his task with apprehension. He was sure that people were distracted from serious reading and their minds turned to a "hodge-podge" by too much eclectic lecture-going. Worried, too, that audiences accustomed to being wooed and flattered by "showy" speakers would find him dull, he actually risked insulting them when he said: "Too much is brought down to the common mind—popularized, as they phraze [*sic*] it—instead of the common mind being elevated to it, or left, for its own good, to reverence where it does not clearly comprehend:— nothing goes on slowly, thoughtfully, silently, alone. This is vitiating the mind more than most people are aware of, or, if aware, more than they have the independence or willingness to confess."[33] If somewhat impolitic, this high-minded severity was at least in keeping with his message that literature since the age of Shakespeare had undergone a steady decline.

Literature, Dana argued, could not fare well in a society in which many were still convinced that works of the imagination were at best frivolous lies and at worst a moral danger. Yet this mistrust of works of the imagination was the legacy of the Scottish commonsense philosophers. In his first lecture, Dana delivered a romantic defense of literature, explaining why there is nothing more important and real than poetry. The highest truths, he said, come not through the fragmentary, limited, and imperfect world of our everyday existence but through the imagination. It is the imagination that sets us free from depraved tastes, grave worldiness, and "hankerings for all that cloys." It woos us from the "dark recesses and passages of Mammon's cave."[34] Through the contemplation of literature, we can strengthen our spiritual life. He said we must look to poetry to "give expanse to our imagination, activity to our fancy, to open the passages deep down into our natures, to unseal our eyes to the beauty, grandeur, and secret spiritual meanings of the outer world, and to make us feel the correspondence between the outer world, and our inner selves."[35] Because receptivity to literature is a measure of individual and national virtue, indifference to it is a serious matter. In his second lecture, Dana explained why seventeenth-century England inspired her writers to greatness while America seemed to crush hers. He believed that in Shakespeare's time the individual and the poet were one. Ordinary life blended imperceptibly into the poetic. The world gave delight without requiring a radical transformation by the imagination. Since no gulf existed between nature and culture, the poet did not feel forced to choose between the two. In the nineteenth century, however, poets are not drawn to nature out of sympathy but driven to her as a refuge. Repeating a point that he had made in his Independence Day oration, Dana stated that because poets find no diversity in the society around them, they are easily "blurred into the tame, monotonous hue of the mass."[36] In the age of Shakespeare, people were filled with awe and wonder at a world so inexplicable that witches and dragons were not beyond belief; but in the skeptical nineteenth century, the world had become dis-enchanted by the conviction that "nothing can be but what may be comprehended—nothing is but what is known."[37] He feared that writers would never again possess the naturalness, simplicity, vitality, and spiritual wisdom of a Shakespeare. Their work would be self-conscious and affected, marred by egotism and metaphysical pretensions.

Dana's allegiance to romanticism was nowhere more apparent than in his unqualified admiration for Shakespeare. English neoclassical critics had revered Shakespeare, but they were so preoccupied with defending him against the charges of ignorance, superstition, and barbarism made by French critics and so committed to the concept of universal rules that their analyses tended to be qualified and lukewarm. They weighed defects against "beauties," criticizing Shakespeare for neglecting the dramatic unities while praising him for his insight into the universal condition of man. The romantic critics August Schlegel and Samuel Coleridge introduced new principles for evaluating and appreciating Shakespeare's plays. Coleridge's lectures on Shakespeare were not published until after his death. What Dana knew of Coleridge's views was gleaned from his reading of *The Friend*. Dana introduced his American audiences to a romantic version of Shakespeare. In several lectures, he tried to show listeners reared on the neoclassical critics John Dryden and Samuel Johnson that Shakespeare was no undisciplined genius but a consummate poet of the imagination, whose profound insights into the human psyche gave his plays a greater integrity than any observance of formal rules of dramatic composition could have achieved.

Dana explained to his audiences that it was a mistake to judge a work of literature by rules invented in a different time and place. The greater vitality, daring, and imagination, the deeper feelings and spiritual resources of Shakespeare's time demanded a drama different from that envisioned by Aristotle. If every age places its stamp on a writer's work, thereby making universal rules impossible, it does not follow that the truth of a work is limited to its time. The real genius of Shakespeare, Dana argued, was his ability to reveal unchanging truths about humanity through the actions and words of unique, highly individualized characters. Shakespeare was the master of the unity to be found in variety, the poet who most successfully revealed the truth that "the atom mystically contains the universe."[38] It was Shakespeare's ability to reconcile the universal and the particular that, in Dana's view, prevented his supernatural characters, such as Ariel or Caliban in *The Tempest,* from seeming improbable or outlandish.

Neoclassical critics, who believed that the object of art is to represent nature faithfully (or to represent the universal in human experience), were troubled by such characters. To the extent that an Ariel or a Caliban could not be found "in nature" they were thought to be "intolerable." Dryden justified a character like Caliban by arguing that, like the centaur, he was a composite of familiar elements. For romantic critics like Coleridge and Dana, however, "supernatural characters" did not have to meet the test of existence but of psychological truthfulness. Dana admired Shakespeare's witches, faeries, and hobgoblins for the wonderfully surprising ways in which they revealed human feelings and follies. Though Caliban is a monster and "of the earth, earthy," and though he lacks a moral will, he has feelings that we recognize as our own. Dana believed that we behold our kinship because Shakespeare, without ever compromising the characteristics of Caliban as a monster, endows him with a sensitivity to music and an ability to express himself in the universal language of natural imagery. Dana was convinced that the dramatic representation of the supernatural was greatly needed in an age too inclined to believe that "nothing is but what is known." Dana explained, "It is not so much, then, that the marvellous is brought down to our natures and to the condition and shape of the world around us, as that our ordinary natures and, with these, our hitherto undeveloped faculties are borne upward, along with this gross, material world, into the superior regions of the poet's fancy."[39] Shakespeare humanizes the monster Caliban and spiritually elevates all who see his plays by making them sharers in his imaginative powers.

Dana had no patience with critics and audiences who felt that Shakespeare's depiction of violence and death on stage showed a lack of refinement. In his fourth lecture, he took up this issue, arguing that "there is but little which may not be rendered a fit subject for scenic representation, if great genius, with its attendent judgment, go to the work."[40] A playwright's efforts to ensure the audience's identification with the characters may require that bloody deeds be enacted on stage. If we are to feel the passions and sorrows of a Hamlet or a Macbeth, we must, Dana insisted, be made a party to his fate. We must be made to feel the suffering of those who suffer. It is not that we crave the excitement of murder, but rather that "our sympathetic natures cry out for the last dark deed . . . that we may feel more and more intensely with him, and mourn over him with the deeper sorrow as he lies dead before us."[41] In the absence of such tragic resolutions, we feel that something is amiss, some betrayal of the principles of cause and effect, some abrogation of our part in the play's action. If the great wrongs done to or by the characters were wholly alien to us, then we might feel that such violence was gratuitous. But, said Dana, Shakespeare's greatness lies in his understanding that we are all kindred spirits, even with the murderer Macbeth. We are not shocked by such acts because we know them to be the outward expressions of inward states of mind, the "tongues by which the inner language becomes audible to our ears."[42]

Murder was not the only "painful and offensive act" in Shakespeare's plays to which critics and audiences objected. In the nineteenth century some critics, including Coleridge, were troubled by the interracial marriage of Desdemona and Othello. Dana, however, was less bothered by the racial issue than by the improbability of Desdemona's love for a man whose claim to her affection was his military valor. Such a love seemed to violate the stereotype of women as delicate, innocent, and pure. Unaware that this exaggerated view of femininity was a product of nineteenth-century historical forces, Dana set out, in his fifth lecture, to prove that Shakespeare had not done violence to women's nature when he cast Desdemona in the role of the warrior Othello's lover. Acknowledging that Desdemona possesses a passionate nature, Dana insisted that her love for Othello is "purified into spiritual essences." To explain how one so spiritual could be drawn to the bold and ardent Othello, Dana introduced the Platonic idea that every individual is a half of some yearned-for whole, longing for a soul mate who will complement his or her being. The woman who most fully embodies the ideal of the feminine principle is most attracted to the man who actualizes the ideal masculine type, for his qualities are those she lacks. No one should be offended by their love, Dana argued, since Desdemona is Othello's true complement; her love for him is not evidence of servility, self-sacrificing subordination, or indecent passion but represents the appropriate though tragic uniting of two heroic natures.

In his sixth lecture, Dana used these same Platonic ideas to bolster his attack on the women's rights movement. The lecture had nothing to do with Shakespeare or literature. Like many nineteenth-century lecturers, Dana swerved from his declared course to offer quite personal reflections on incidental topics. The notion of equal rights for women filled him with horror. The results, he exclaimed, would be "monstrous, monstrous." He argued that the fullness of creation and the perfection of the social state require the subordination of women. Women who usurp the place of men, like poor men who aspire to the positions of the better sort, defy the divine order of things by lessening diversity. As Othello needs Desdemona to be fully human, so society requires a complementary interdependency between men and women "in order to bring out humankind in its many possible individual varieties . . . till the sum of all these, the Social State, becomes the representative and incorporation of Entire Man."[43] Women must remain faithful to the attributes and responsibilities of their sex. A woman's strength, Dana insisted, lies in "persuasive, beseeching gentleness," her courage lies in her endurance, and her intelligence arises from affection.[44] Any woman who does not derive joy from reverencing a man as her superior, he suggested, is not only "wanting in the highest essentials of her feminine nature," but probably lacking in a due reverence for God as well.

Dana's appreciation of Shakespeare's plays was evident in his first five lectures, but he had said nothing as yet that was particularly original. For the most part, he had treated the plays as a backdrop before which he marshaled his attack on the superficiality and stupefying utilitarianism of American culture. He had drawn an attractive portrait of the diversity and spiritual richness of Shakespeare's time as a way of revealing the thinness of America in his own. Contempt for American prudery and squeamishness, as well as for the persistence of neoclassical critical values, animated his defense of Shakespeare's use of the supernatural and the violent. In his last lectures, which were on *Hamlet* and *Macbeth,* Dana offered a sustained analysis of the characters of the two heroes. These highly personal, even idiosyncratic lectures reveal again the depth of his preoccupation with romantic themes. He saw something of himself in Hamlet, and interpreted both plays as dramatizations of the problematic nature of the creative imagination. Both Hamlet and Macbeth, he insisted, were victims of intense, overwrought imaginations and were brought to tragic ends by their misdirected longings for the absolute.

Most romantic critics were moved by the "prince of philosophical speculators," as Hazlitt called Hamlet. Dana's reading of the play bore a strong family resemblance to the criticism of Schlegel, Coleridge, and Hazlitt. He too stressed the meditative, abstract cast of Hamlet's mind. But while they were concerned with showing how the actions of the play reveal the moral consequences of such an imbalance between the active and the meditative faculties, Dana sought to demonstrate Shakespeare's understanding of the poetic imagination. Dana viewed Hamlet as the quintessential romantic poet.

Hamlet fails to act because he is a philosophical idealist whose inner world, a world created by the spiritualizing, refining, and transforming power of the imagination, is more compelling and real than the shadowy, fearful world of everyday experience. Grief over the murder of his father and the sins of a mother "worse than dead" have led him to prefer the imaginary to the real. His treatment of Ophelia, which critic Samuel Johnson thought wanton and cruel, was, Dana argued, perfectly consistent with this idealism. Even this love is more imagined than real. First conceived as an ideal in his mind, the image of perfect love is more real to Hamlet than the flesh and blood woman before him. He tests Ophelia, not out of unkindness, but to reassure himself of the depth of her love.

Hamlet's tormented, ambiguous love for Ophelia is but one expression of his far deeper longing to experience to the fullest all the possibilities of mind and imagination—to become the "infinite self." The soul, through the power of the imagination, desires to know the extent of its powers. Knowing itself to be finite, but sprung from the infinite, the soul struggles to realize that infinite. According to Dana, "the living soul hungers and thirsts to experience its all of being."[45] He added: "Realizing nothing without, it must strive to realize all of self, and more than self within; and, to this end, must push every faculty and emotion to the very verge of its being: the more of conscious, inward sense, the more the assurance of life. In this alone is its life, its reality."[46] Dana argued that it is this Faustian ambition to push to the verge of being that accounts both for Hamlet's apparent cruelty and for his feigned insanity. Dana apparently saw Hamlet as an example of Coleridge's observation that men of great imaginative powers are often tempted to walk the narrow line between sanity and madness. Recognizing the affinity between the imagination and lunacy, such individuals crave "only to hover in that fearful twilight region betwixt sanity and madness. . . . All short of it is tame and palling."[47]

We are not dealing here with Shakespeare's tragic prince but with Dana's "ideal poet" and with his convictions about the powerful attractions and terrible dangers of the creative imagination. He is describing his own Paul Felton, not Shakespeare's Hamlet. T. S. Eliot once said that the psychological critics of the nineteenth century (Goethe and Coleridge) found in Hamlet "a vicarious existence for their own artistic realization." This is certainly true of Dana as well. In his reading of *Hamlet,* it is not some tragic incongruity between the demands of the moment and Hamlet's character that poses the dramatic problem of the play. Rather, Dana said of Hamlet, as he might have said of himself, "This world was not made for him to act in, or he formed to act in it."[48] Possessing a temperament too refined for the times in which he lives, Hamlet acts, Dana argued, according to principles appropriate to the eternal world to which "he is soon to be translated," where thoughts are actions and the inward life is sufficient. The play affirmed the same Christian "truths" that Dana had learned from his own struggle with the subjectivity of the imagination. He told his audiences that only union with God could gratify the longing for being and free the soul from the rack of passions.

Dana's most original observations on Shakespeare's plays were made in his lecture on *Macbeth.* He found more depth to Macbeth's character than did most contemporary critics. Coleridge's Macbeth is an ambitious, selfish, and calculating hypocrite; Hazlitt viewed him as a man of noble possibilities seduced by "golden opportunity" and dominated by his stronger, wickedly magnificent wife. Dana, on the other hand, saw in Macbeth's character the same Faustian longing for majesty that moved Hamlet. Impelled by a powerful imagination, Macbeth is thrust beyond "the circle of the merely human" not by tawdry ambition but by a distorted vision of the possibilities of the self. Dana told his audiences:

[Macbeth's] mind possessed not only the character of greatness, but of that undefined vastness, also, which belongs to the imaginative. . . . He craved to realize to himself what this spirit of majesty might be—to possess majesty that he might be possessed by it—might make this abstraction, living, individual consciousness within him. Only to bow before the throne of this magnific God of his idolatry was too distant and distinct from self:—he would fain ascend his throne, and become one with him in spirit, and thus realize by appropriation that which he so adored.[49]

Dana viewed Macbeth as a man whose longing for the good has been tragically perverted. This interpretation bears the telltale marks of his Christian Platonism. He believed that dreams of greatness, the ambition to live to the full extent of one's power, are manifestations of a yearning for union with God. For Dana the universality of *Macbeth,* and its moral persuasiveness, arose out of Shakespeare's representation of the eternal struggle of "half-freed powers" "to work their way to entire life."[50] The imagination is one such power. When inspired by God, it is the source of delight and truth; when alienated from the divine, it is a fountain of horror and evil.

Macbeth's imagination provides the key to both his nobility and his wickedness. It animates his moral sense and it goads him on to further crimes. His conscience speaks to him through his imagination. By evoking Duncan's virtues and bringing before his mind's eye images of bloody dagger and aggrieved ghost, Macbeth intensifies his remorse. Coleridge thought these whisperings of conscience insignificant because they are so promptly translated into prudential and selfish reasonings. But Dana, who was convinced of the complexity of Macbeth's character, insisted that his torment and remorse were real. In the end, Dana argued, Macbeth's imagination must slay his conscience in order to secure the majesty and power his soul craves. It goads him on by painting his character and deeds in the most lurid colors; through the power of image and language Macbeth's imagination crushes his remorse, intensifies his terror, and drives him forward. The play demonstrated Dana's own belief about the characters of greatly wicked people: the noble parts of their natures are made the servants of their evil passions. Thus, if Macbeth's imagination had been less powerful and his nature less kind, Dana observed, he would have been more at ease in his crimes.[51]

In Macbeth's relationship with the witches, Dana found further evidence of Shakespeare's insight into the operations of the imagination. The witches are not simply agents of evil who play upon Macbeth's ambition. They appeal instead to his imagination and thus broaden out the moral landscape in which he acts. By linking his deeds to a supernatural realm in which acts are decreed by Fate, the witches impart an element of the sublime to Macbeth's crimes. In his transaction with the witches, Macbeth "is transformed to more than man; thus, in union with the supernatural, the invisible and infinite, his being, as it were, expands into them and he becomes of them. The laws of earth and of his fellow-creatures are too low and narrow to be longer his rule—mind, his mind, overshadows them."[52] In other words, the witches appeal to Macbeth's imagination when they intimate that all of nature—fate itself—backs his longing to exceed human limits.

Dana's preoccupation with the aesthetic and metaphysical implications of the creative imagination dominated his analysis and, to some extent, distorted his perceptions of Macbeth's character. Macbeth's imagination is narrower in scope and less transcendental in its aspiration than Dana believed. Nevertheless, Dana did better than most of his contemporaries in suggesting the complexity of Macbeth's motivations and the tensions within his character. He believed that from these conflicts rose the meditative mood that, in the last act, "touches and softens the black deeds of his hand" with qualities of mind and soul.[53] Dana was convinced that *Macbeth* more than *Hamlet* revealed the depth of Shakespeare's insight into the moral nature of humankind. His cousin Edward T. Channing took the more popular view when he declared that *Macbeth* was unworthy of Shakespeare.[54]

Late in 1847 the publishers Baker & Scribner urged Dana to include his lectures on Shakespeare in the edition of his collected works that they were planning to publish. Hoping to take advantage of the growing interest in Shakespeare, they expected the lectures to increase sales. But Dana refused. Perhaps he resisted because publication would cost him a reliable source of income; perhaps he felt that he would have to make major revisions. Dana already had an impressive younger rival in Henry Norman Hudson, whose two volumes of *Lectures on Shakespeare* were scheduled for publication in 1848. Dana also may have sensed that his lectures were dated. His attacks upon the neoclassical critics Dryden and Johnson were, by 1848, mere echoes of battles waged and won at least a decade before. Several of the lectures, especially those on Desdemona and on woman, were abstract, prolix, and boring. The humor, imagery, and sinewy Anglo-Saxon phrasing so present in his earlier reviews were missing. Unrevised, the lectures would not have stood up to a comparison with Coleridge, Hazlitt, or Hudson.

And yet they were not without merit. When first delivered in 1838, they made an important contribution to enhancing the appreciation and understanding of Shakespeare. Margaret Fuller, who was a member of the transcendentalist circle and an outstanding literary critic, had been present at that first series of lectures delivered in Providence. She was also familiar with the "inspired" and erratic Jones Very's essay on *Hamlet*. She reported to Emerson that she much preferred Dana's. "Mr. Very," she wrote, "is *infinitely* inferior in accuracy of perception to Mr. Dana, and has not so much insight, but he soars higher."[55] The lectures on *Hamlet* and *Macbeth* were original, thoughtful, and interesting examples of romantic Shakespearean criticism. They reveal what Dana might have done had he seriously undertaken a thorough study of the plays; but he was too distracted by his profound disillusionment with American society and culture and too preoccupied with probing the possibilities of the imagination to focus his attention squarely on Shakespeare's work.

Though Dana decided not to include the lectures, Baker & Scribner went ahead with the publication of his collected works in the winter of 1849–50. The two-volume *Poems and Prose Writings* included the *Idle Man*, *The Buccaneer* and a few additional poems, his essays, and all but two of the review articles that he had written over the years for the *North American Review*, the *Spirit of the Pilgrims*, and other periodicals. Dana insisted that this time he felt indifferent to sales figures and critical responses, much as a cow toward its weaned calf.[56] There were the usual disappointments. Several periodicals gave his work only a perfunctory short announcement, promising a more thorough treatment later. He discussed with his son the possibility of Hudson's reviewing the work for the *North American Review* but, for obscure reasons, this idea came to nothing. Bryant declined to rally to the cause, protesting quite reasonably that he had already said all that he could. Sales were slow, but not all was disappointing. Two reviews were not merely just but perceptive and admiring. George Washington Peck, whose essay appeared in the *American Whig Review*, and Edwin Percy Whipple, whose review was published by the *Christian Examiner*, described Dana as a major American writer of great intelligence, imagination, profound feeling, and moral earnestness.[57]

Peck described Dana as a "genius soaring with fettered wings."[58] Taking "The Buccaneer" as an example of both Dana's strengths and weaknesses as a poet, Peck praised its originality and the way the highly dramatic narrative and the beautiful, lyrical descriptions of the shoreline scenery were integrated into a harmonious whole. But, he added, "the most remarkable quality to us in it, is the power with which it is carried through over a very rough and jagged roadway of style."[59] He explained why Dana had never become a popular writer. The poems, he argued, expressed feelings with which most people (he pointedly excluded himself) could not identify—love so intense, delicate, and overwhelming that lovers were driven mad; suffering so deep and obscure in origin that the common reader felt only baffled or impatient. It was Dana's Calvinism with all its gloom, self-torment, and despair that, according to Peck, accounted for the harshness of his vision and the stifled quality of his verse. "They will understand him best," he observed, "who have groped their way through the peculiar gloom of New England Calvinism."[60] He described Paul Felton as a "Puritan Hamlet," and Dana as one who "has fought through the mental diseases entailed upon the descendants of the Puritans."

His remarks on "Paul Felton" were suffused with the condescension that the high-spirited literary set in New York felt for Boston's more sober men of letters. Peck could not resist tossing a few partisan barbs at Bostonians: "There they go about like Athenians of old, inquiring for new things and new religions," (this was hardly true of Dana!) and taxing each other with such observations as: "You say this, because you fancy I said that, because you said the other. . . ."[61] Peck's notion that Dana's genius had been fettered by Calvinism was to become the prevailing opinion among critics. While it is true that Dana was influenced by Calvinist ideas, Peck oversimplified the complexity of his vision by reducing it to this one element. As originally conceived, Felton was not a Puritan but a crazed romantic poet. The harshness of Dana's outlook was not due simply to his belief that man is a fallen being but to his temperament, his disgust with the culture of democracy, and his personal disappointments and tragedy. Insensitive to the beliefs and attitudes that offset this harshness, Peck did not do justice to Dana's love of nature and beauty or to the Platonism that had enabled him to believe at last in the goodness that lies at the heart of creation. Upon reading Peck's review, Dana quite properly remarked that his opinions were "monomaniacal."[62]

Of all the critics who discussed Dana's work, Edwin P. Whipple came the closest to explaining why Dana had failed to become a first-rate writer. A personal friend of Richard Henry Dana, Jr., Whipple was an intelligent, self-taught literary critic and a shrewd, sensitive observer of character. In his review, he set out to explain how the "most original of American poets" and "one of our deepest and most suggestive thinkers" had fallen so far short of his original promise. Like Peck, Whipple sensed that Dana had written under some overwhelming sense of constraint. Dana's work, Whipple wrote, lacked freedom, audacity of manner, and spontaneity. It possessed nervous energy, imagination, and intelligence in abundance but no great force or power. Although capable of a "Chaucerian certainty in representing a natural object in its exact form, color, and dimensions" and of an exquisite melodiousness of expression (more often in prose than in poetry, where Dana's faults were a "willful defect"), Dana was unable to integrate feeling and thought into a sustained release of creativity.[63] Whipple understood that Dana was constrained by a deep conflict in his personality, by self-doubt, and by a profoundly ingrained disgust with the world. "His finer affections, the saint-like purity of his moral feelings, the sentiments of awe, wonder, reverence, and beauty incorporated with his religious faith" were, Whipple argued, all at war with an equally deep hostility toward society and perhaps toward humankind.[64] He suggested that Dana's real power had been drained away in scorn, a cool, refined contempt, and unending self-distrust. It had been Dana's misfortune to be always in opposition: "This moral fastidiousness of a strong moral nature, this mental disgust 'sickling o'er' the energies of a great mind, . . . must be accounted for principally by the fact that Mr. Dana's life has been one of antagonism to the tastes and opinions of the community in which he was placed."[65] If Dana had received the recognition that the "depth and richness of his mind" warranted and his shy and sensitive nature craved, then *Poems and Prose Writings,* Whipple asserted, "would hardly have been a tithe of his contributions to literature."[66]

Allowing for a certain overfriendliness in Whipple's judgment, there is a great deal of truth in his views. We have only to compare Dana's impressive review of Hazlitt's *Lectures on the English Poets* with his lectures on Shakespeare to sense the toll taken by this adversarial relationship to the world. The intelligence and earnestness remain but not the high spirits or the sense of a man fully enjoying the powers of his mind and spirit. Whipple recognized that a part of Dana's tragedy was to have been born before his time. When Dana was at the height of his powers, Whipple observed, romantic views were treated disdainfully like "freaks of spiritual caprice." By 1850, they excited "nothing more than respect and admiration for the thinker."[67]

Father and Son

Dana's modest income from lecturing eased the family's troubled finances, but it was his son Richard Henry, Jr., who was largely responsible for restoring an even keel. A brisk, socially ambitious, and energetic man, the younger Dana was acutely embarrassed by the family's poverty. While his father withered under the strain of adversity, he was galvanized into activity. After his two years before the mast, the younger Dana completed his Harvard degree and attended the Dane Law School. He then established a law practice and took over the management of the family lands. He collected the rents and sold some of the land at a profit. Although he was too careless in his investments and too extravagant to succeed in his dream of recovering the splendor of his grandfather's time, he did do well enough to provide amply for his own family and to ensure his father a secure old age. In 1845 he purchased a summer home at Cape Ann. The estate stood on a bluff overlooking the ocean. For the elder Dana, it was a dream come true—a refuge from the heat and congestion of Boston and a source of much pleasure. He told his son that "the owning of it would be almost too much delight for him to enjoy."[68]

The relationship between Dana and his son has provoked comment from biographers and scholars who have studied the life and work of the younger man. The comments have rarely been flattering to the father. Characterized as an idle, hypochondriacal, and morose misfit, the elder Dana appears as an incubus, oppressing his son with querulous demands, morbid anxieties, and old resentments. Of course there is some truth in these observations. He was often melancholy, ill, and depressed. At his worst moments, Dana sank into a lethargy that caused his family a good deal of distress.

The younger Dana tried to purge himself of the qualities he disliked in his father. He prided himself on his physical vitality and courage and on his competence in worldly, practical affairs; yet, it was his father who, knowing the price of timidity and hypersensitivity, fought down the impulse to protect his son from the dangers of boyhood and encouraged him in his hardy, self-reliant ways. Although he felt a father's anxiety when his son set out on his two year voyage before the mast, he did not, as some have suggested, try to discourage the adventure. In fact, he envied his son. In a letter to Mrs. Arnold, he commented: "Still, I feel that it will confirm him in an energetic & independent character; & in the midst of my anxiety for him, I cannot help exclaiming, O, that I had been thus thrown upon the world young as he, then should I have not been torn in pieces by an over sensitive nature, & have starved my life long, on faint & disappointed hopes."[69]

In his battle for self-definition, the younger Dana may have underestimated how much he owed his father. He seems to have adopted many of his father's opinions about literary and religious issues and, though not the monarchist his father professed to be, held similarly conservative political views. He had his father's moral courage but not his depth, his searching intelligence, or his openness to new ideas. While the elder Dana was prepared to rethink some of his religious and literary ideas, the younger man seems to have held fast to the positions that he felt were most consistent with his class and worldly ambitions.

Father and son were bound together by a mutual respect and love that outweighed any tensions and resentments. In spite of his busy schedule, the younger Dana tried in many ways to help his father meet his obligations and reap praise and profit from his years of writing and reflection. After Washington Allston's death in 1843, Richard, Jr., assisted his father in gathering materials for a biographical memoir. He set up the successful Philadelphia lecture series and, when the elder Dana's collected works were published in 1849, sent out the review copies and tried to secure competent, sympathetic reviewers. For his part, the elder Dana took great pride in his son's success as a writer, an attorney, and an antislavery man. When he first read the manuscript of *Two Years Before the Mast,* Dana recognized all the hallmarks of an impressive achievement in the book's simplicity, originality, and graphic descriptions. He helped edit and find a publisher for his son's manuscript.

When he died in 1879 at the age of ninety-two, Dana and his work had been long forgotten. To the religious and philosophical critics of Darwinism, Dana's battles against the earlier champions of scientific empiricism and common sense meant as little as fossile trilobites. His Christian romanticism won no followers among the romanticists of the American Renaissance. He was no one's precursor. Dana was neither surprised nor embittered by an obscurity he had anticipated. Soon after the publication of *Two Years Before the Mast,* people began stopping him in the street to congratulate him on his son's success. He reported the incidents to Bryant, and without a trace of regret commented, "I expect to be henceforth spoken of as the father of the writer of *Two Years Before the Mast.*"[70]

Notes and References

Chapter One

1. Samuel Shapiro, *Richard Henry Dana, Jr.: 1815–1882* (East Lansing: Michigan State University Press, 1961), 3.
2. Edward T. Channing, *Life of William Ellery,* vol. 6 of *The Library of American Biography,* ed. Jared Sparks (New York: Harper & Brothers, 1848), 156.
3. Ibid.
4. Andrew Peabody, *Harvard Reminiscences* (Freeport, N.Y.: Books for Libraries Press, 1972), 37–38.
5. Richard Henry Dana to Caleb Sprague Henry, 27 December 1834, Dana Papers, Massachusetts Historical Society.
6. Correspondent Philo-Mathesis, "Strictures on the Literary Exhibitions of the Students in Harvard College," *Monthly Anthology* I (December 1803): 58–59. Kenneth Silverman discusses the popularity of a cult of sentimentality among American undergraduates in the 1790s in *A Cultural History of the American Revolution* (New York: Thomas Y. Crowell, 1976), 590–91.
7. J. B. Flagg, *Life and Letters of Washington Allston* (New York: Charles Scribner's Sons, 1897), 27–28. The term *Sturm und Drang* refers to a literary movement in late eighteenth-century Germany that was characterized by a fervent nationalism and by the portrayal of intense emotional and spiritual struggles.
8. Lewis P. Simpson, "A Literary Adventure of the Early Republic: The Anthology Society and the *Monthly Anthology,*" *New England Quarterly* 27 (January 1954): 189–90.
9. Arthur Maynard Walter, "Our Country," *Monthly Anthology* (September 1807): 472. Although Walter was not a conservative, his evaluation is typical of the members' tendency to disparage the work of the revolutionary generation.
10. Joseph Stevens Buckminster, "Remarker," *Monthly Anthology* 5 (July 1808):368.
11. Ibid., 369.
12. Samuel Thacher, "American Poetry," *Monthly Anthology* 2 (September 1805):460.
13. Joseph Stevens Buckminster, "The Dangers and Duties of Men of Letters," *Monthly Anthology* 7 (September 1809):145–58.
14. Joseph Stevens Buckminster, "Remarker," *Monthly Anthology* 3 (January 1806):22.

15. Theodore Dehon, "Phi Beta Kappa Discourse," *Monthly Anthology* 4 (September 1807):472.

16. Edmund Dana, "The Powers of Genius," *Monthly Anthology* 2 (October 1805):530.

17. Benjamin Welles, "Remarker," *Monthly Anthology* 3 (June 1806):285, 286.

18. Ibid., 285.

19. Arthur Maynard Walter, "On Pope," *Monthly Anthology* 2 (May 1805): 236.

20. Edmund Dana, "Review of Linn's The Powers of Genius," *Monthly Anthology* 2 (October 1805):531.

21. Ibid., 532.

22. Ibid., 533.

23. Richard Henry Dana to William A. Jones, 3 June 1850, Dana Papers, Massachusetts Historical Society.

24. William Ellery to Dana, 23 February 1805, Dana Papers.

25. Dana to Martha Dana, October 1807, Dana Papers.

26. Ellery to Martha Dana, May 1 1808, Dana Papers.

27. Edward T. Channing to Dana, 17 February 1812, Dana Papers.

28. Dana to Martha Dana, 24 January 1812, Dana Papers.

29. Dana to Channing, 12 November 1812, Dana Papers.

30. Richard Henry Dana, *Oration Delivered before the Washington Benevolent Society* (Cambridge: Hilliard & Metcalf, 1814), 9.

31. Ibid., 8.

32. Ibid., 7.

33. Ibid., 6.

34. Ibid., 3.

35. Channing to Dana, 14 October 1812, Dana Papers.

Chapter Two

1. Richard Henry Dana, *Poems and Prose Writings,* vol. 2, 2d ed. (New York: Baker & Scribner, 1850), 418.

2. Archibald Alison, *Essays in the Nature and Principles of Taste,* 2 vols. (Edinburg: A. Constable & Co., 1825). The *Essays* were first published in 1790 but probably remained unfamiliar to American readers until reviewed by Francis Jeffrey in the *Edinburgh Review* in 1810. An American edition of the *Essays* was published in Boston in 1812.

3. William Charvat, *The Origins of American Critical Thought* (New York: A. S. Barnes & Co., Perpetua Books, 1961), 48.

4. Alison, *Essays* 1:100, 2:433–34.

5. Ibid., 2:437.

6. In his preface to *Poems and Prose Writings* 2:151, Dana declared Wordsworth the most important poet of his age.

7. Richard Henry Dana, "Hazlitt's English Poets," *North American Review* 8 (March 1819):319.

8. William James, "The Present Dilemma in Philosophy," in *Pragmatism and Four Essays from "The Meaning of Truth"* (New York: Meridian Books, 1955), 17–18.

9. The phrase is Dana's. It appears in his review "Hazlitt's English Poets," *North American Review* 8 (March 1819):279.

10. Richard Henry Dana, "Radcliffe's Gaston de Blondeville," *United States Review and Literary Gazette* 2 (April 1827):7.

11. Lewis P. Simpson, *The Federalist Literary Mind: Selections from the Monthly Anthology and Boston Review, 1803–1811, Including Documents Relating to the Boston Athenum* (Baton Rouge: Louisiana State University Press, 1962):12–14.

12. Edward T. Channing to Willard Phillips, 14 August 1852, Phillips Papers, Massachusetts Historical Society.

13. William Ellery to Richard Henry Dana, 26 March 1815, Dana Papers, Massachusetts Historical Society.

14. Channing to Phillips, 14 August 1852, Phillips Papers.

15. Nathan Hale was owner and editor of the *Boston Daily Advertiser* (Boston's major commercial newspaper) and a brother-in-law of Edward Everett. John Gallison and William Mason were attorneys. Willard Phillips later became a prominent lawyer, judge of Suffolk County Probate Court, and an authority on insurance and patent law.

16. Dana to Ellery, 4 June 1817, Dana Papers.

17. Robert Streeter, "Association Psychology and Literary Nationalism in the *North American Review*," *American Literature* 17 (November 1945):246.

18. Edward T. Channing, "On Models in Literature," *North American Review* 3 (July 1816):207.

19. Neal Frank Doubleday, "Doctrines for Fiction in the *North American Review*, 1815–1826," in *Literature and Ideas in America: Essays in Memory of Harry Hayden Clark*, ed. Robert Falk (Columbus: Ohio University Press, 1975), 20–39.

20. Richard Henry Dana, "Irving's Sketch Book," *North American Review* 9 (September 1819):325.

21. Richard Henry Dana, "Allston's Sylphs of the Seasons," *North American Review* 5 (September 1817):366.

22. Dana, "Irving's Sketch Book," 327, 330.

23. Ibid., 331.

24. Dana, "Hazlitt's English Poets," 280.

25. Edward T. Channing, "Rob Roy," *North American Review* 7 (May 1818):155; "The Life of Charles Brockden Brown," *North American Review* 4 (June 1819):74.

26. Willard Phillips, "Review of 'Harrington, A Tale' and 'Ormond, A Tale' by Maria Edgeworth," *North American Review* 6 (January 1818):155; "Lord Byron's 'Childe Harold'," *North American Review* 5 (May 1817):99.

27. Richard Henry Dana, "Old Times," *North American Review* 5 (May 1817):10.
28. Ibid., 8.
29. Dana, "Allston's Sylphs of the Seasons," 370, 384.
30. Ibid., 368.
31. Ibid., 370–71.
32. Richard Henry Dana, "Edgeworths' Readings in Poetry," *North American Review* 8 (May 1818):71.
33. Ibid., 72.
34. Ibid., 73.
35. Ibid., 76.
36. William Hazlitt, *Collected Works,* vol. 2, centenary ed. 113, cited in Herschel Baker, *William Hazlitt* (Cambridge: Belknap Press of Harvard University Press, 1962), 186.
37. Dana, "Hazlitt's English Poets," 290–91.
38. Ibid., 295.
39. Ibid., 301.
40. William Hazlitt, *Lectures on the English Poets* (New York: E. P. Dutton & Co., 1910), 98.
41. Dana, "Hazlitt's English Poets," 281.
42. Ibid., 321.
43. Dana, "Irving's Sketch Book," 348.
44. William L. Hedges, *Washington Irving: An American Study, 1802–1832* (Baltimore: Johns Hopkins Press, 1965), 56.
45. Dana, "Irving's Sketch Book," 334.
46. *Federal Republic and Baltimore Telegraph,* 27 April 1819.
47. Rufus Griswold, *Readings in American Poetry for the Use of Schools* (New York: J. C. Riker, 1843), 111.
48. Dana to Ellery, 31 March 1819, Dana Papers.
49. Henry Adams, *The United States in 1800* (Ithaca, N.Y.: Cornell University Press, 1957), 54.
50. James Grant Wilson, *Bryant and His Friends: Some Reminiscences of the Knickerbocker Writers* (New York: Ford, Howard & Hulbert, 1886), 189.

Chapter Three

1. Bryant contributed four poems to the *Idle Man:* "Green River," "A Walk at Sunset," "A Winter Piece," and "The West Wind." Allston wrote "The Hypochondriac" and "Written in Spring." While a member of the association of contributors to the *North American Review,* Dana had been impressed by a handful of poems submitted by Bryant. Their friendship, which began in 1820, lasted until Bryant's death in 1878. The identity of "the idle man" was soon discovered. The associates of the *North American Review* were not deceived by the Irvingesque format or by Dana's precautions. He re-

ported to Wiley: "They said they knew me well enough from a resemblance to my reviews of Hazlitt, the Sketch Book etc. in the N.A. Review." Richard Henry Dana to Charles Wiley, 2 July 1821, Dana Papers, Massachusetts Historical Society.

2. For a discussion of the conventions of the sentimental novel, see Herbert Ross Brown, *The Sentimental Novel in America* (Durham, N.C.: Duke University Press, 1940).

3. Richard Henry Dana, "Domestic Life," in *Poems and Prose Writings,* vol. 2, 2d ed. (New York: Baker & Scribner, 1850), 428.

4. Ibid., 427.

5. Dana, "The Son," in *Poems and Prose Writings* 2:376.

6. Dana, "Edward and Mary," in *Poems and Prose Writings* 2:223.

7. Ibid., 224.

8. Ibid., 223.

9. Ibid., 266.

10. Dana to William Cullen Bryant, 8 October 1821, Dana Papers, Massachusetts Historical Society.

11. *Columbian Centinel,* 26 May 1821.

12. Ibid., 20 June 1821.

13. *Boston Weekly Messenger,* 28 June 1821.

14. Dana to Bryant, 4 November 1821, Dana Papers.

15. Dana to Bryant, 8 October 1821, Dana Papers.

16. Dana, "Domestic Life," in *Poems and Prose Writings* 2:434.

17. Dana, "Musings," in *Poems and Prose Writings* 2:437–38.

18. Ibid., 438.

19. Ibid., 436.

20. Ibid., 441–42.

21. Ibid., 442–43.

22. Dana to Bryant, November 1821, Dana Papers.

23. William H. Prescott, "Essay Writing," *North American Review* 5 (April 1822):330.

24. Dana, "Thomas Thornton," in *Poems and Prose Writings* 2:164.

25. Dana to Bryant, 9 November 1821, Dana Papers.

26. Richard Henry Dana, Jr., *The Journal of Richard Henry Dana, Jr.,* vol. 1, ed. Robert F. Lucid (Cambridge: Harvard University Press, Belknap Press, 1968), 6.

27. Dana to Bryant, 2 May 1822, Dana Papers.

28. Dana to Bryant, 21 August 1822, Dana Papers.

29. Dana, "Paul Felton," in *Poems and Prose Writings* 2:273.

30. Ibid., 277.

31. Ibid., 274.

32. Ibid., 317–18.

33. Ibid., 312.

34. "Well Wisher," *Columbian Centinel,* 13 November 1822.

35. Willard Phillips to Bryant, 17 February 1822, Bryant-Godwin Collection, New York Public Library.
36. Dana to Bryant, 9 December 1821, Dana Papers.
37. Bryant to Dana, 28 March 1822, Goddard-Roslyn Collection, microfilm 3.
38. *Columbian Centinel,* 27 November 1822.
39. Prescott, "Essay Writing," 330.
40. Letter fragment of Dana's, undated and included in the 1822 folder of the Dana Papers.

Chapter Four

1. Richard Henry Dana to William Cullen Bryant, 20 January 1823, Dana Papers, Massachusetts Historical Society. Dana borrowed the phrase "Lethe ['s] wharf" from *Hamlet,* Act 1, scene 5.
2. The younger Dana viewed his father in this way. When breaking the news of Allston's death, he reassured his aunts that "if it had been some embarrassment or trouble of worldly or pecuniary matters it would make [Dana, Sr.] ill, but that so great a thing as this he could stand up against." *The Journal of Richard Henry Dana, Jr.,* vol. 1, ed. Robert F. Lucid (Cambridge: Harvard University Press, Belknap Press 1968), 172. Samuel Shapiro, in his biography of the younger Dana, not only asserts that Dana was a hypochondriac but also claims that he was senile by the age of fifty, a claim that is singularly unlikely because Dana wrote and delivered a series of successful lectures in the 1840s and conducted an active and informed correspondence until just weeks before his death at the age of ninety-two. *Richard Henry Dana, Jr., 1815–1882* (East Lansing: Michigan State University Press, 1961), 14.
3. Marilyn Butler, *Romantics, Rebels, and Reactionaries: English Literature and its Background, 1760–1830.* (New York and Oxford: Oxford University Press, 1981), 76.
4. Dana to Bryant, 16 November 1824, Dana Papers.
5. Dana to Bryant, 15 April 1825, Dana Papers.
6. Bryant to Dana, 25 May 1825, Goddard-Roslyn Collection, microfilm 3, New York Public Library.
7. Dana to Bryant, 21 June 1825, Dana Papers.
8. Ibid.
9. The poems originally appearing in the *New York Review* included "The Dying Raven," "Fragment of an Epistle," "Little Beach Bird," and "The Husband and Wife's Grave." The new poems were "The Buccaneer," "Changes of Home," "A Clump of Daisies," "The Pleasure Boat," and "Daybreak."
10. Richard Henry Dana, "The Buccaneer," in *Poems and Prose Writings,* vol. 1, 2d ed. (New York: Baker & Scribner, 1850), 5.

11. Ibid., 23.
12. Ibid., 3.
13. Ibid., 24.
14. James McHenry, "Dana's Poems," *American Quarterly Review* 3 (1828):118.
15. Dana, "The Dying Raven," in *Poems and Prose Writings* 1:102.
16. Ibid., 104–5.
17. Ibid., 105.
18. Dana, "Fragment of an Epistle," in *Poems and Prose Writings* 1:108.
19. Dana, "Changes of Home," in *Poems and Prose Writings* 1:38.
20. Ibid., 58.
21. Dana, "The Little Beach Bird," in *Poems and Prose Writings* 1:130.
22. Dana, "Daybreak," in *Poems and Prose Writings* 1:140.
23. Ibid., 142.
24. James McHenry, "Dana's Poems," 126.
25. William Cullen Bryant, "Dana's Poems," *North American Review* 26 (January 1828): 239.
26. Dana to Bryant, 2 November 1827, Dana Papers.
27. William Cullen Bryant, "Lectures on Poetry," in *The Life and Works of William Cullen Bryant,* vol. 3, ed. Parke Godwin (New York: D. Appleton and Co., 1883), 19.
28. Roy Harvey Pearce, *The Continuity of American Poetry* (Princeton, N.J.: Princeton University Press, 1961), 193.
29. Dana's reviews in the *United States Review and Literary Gazette* were "Yorktown," 2 (January 1827); "Radcliffe's Gaston de Blondville," 2 (April, 1827):1–8; and "The Novels of Charles Brockden Brown," 2 (August 1827):321–33.
30. Dana, "The Novels of Charles Brockden Brown," 324.
31. Ibid., 325.
32. Ibid., 328.
33. Ibid., 325.
34. Dana to Sarah Arnold, 4 August 1827, Dana Papers.
35. Charles Folsom to William Cullen Bryant, 11 January 1827, Bryant-Godwin Collection, New York Public Library.
36. Bryant to Folsom, January 1827, Bryant Papers, Boston Public Library.
37. Dana to Bryant, 26 February 1827, Dana Papers.
38. Dana, "Radcliffe's Gaston de Blondville," 3.
39. Dana to Bryant, 8 June 1828, Dana Papers.

Chapter Five

1. The term *Christian romantic* refers to those who insisted that the essence of the religious experience lies in an immediate, intuitive awareness

of God while accepting orthodox Christian doctrines of grace, resurrection, the Trinity, and so on. In Europe the leading voice of Christian romanticism was Friedrich Schleiermacher, in England it was Samuel Coleridge, and in the United States it was James Marsh and Horace Bushnell. Sidney Ahlstrom, *A Religious History of the American People* (New Haven and London: Yale University Press, 1972), 597–614.

2. Lyman Beecher, *The Autobiography*, ed. Barbara M. Cross (Cambridge: Harvard University Press, Belknap Press, 1961), 81. The novelist Harriet Beecher Stowe was Lyman Beecher's daughter.

3. Martin Rugoff, *The Beechers: An American Family in the Nineteenth Century* (New York: Harper & Row, 1981), 64. The younger Dana bears out Rugoff's suggestion that the Unitarians of Boston were so put off by Beecher's manners that they would not take him seriously. Beecher was careless in dress and manner and, according to Richard, Jr., "inattentive to what we had been sedulously taught as the 'Minor Morals'." *The Journal of Richard Henry Dana, Jr.,* vol. 2, ed. Robert F. Lucid (Cambridge: Harvard University Press, Belknap Press, 1968) 518.

4. Richard Henry Dana, *An Account of the Controversy between the First Parish of Cambridge and the Rev. Dr. Holmes, their Late Pastor* (Cambridge, Mass., 1829), 77.

5. Richard Henry Dana, "Men and Books," *Idle Man* 1, no. 4 (1821):13.

6. Richard Henry Dana, "Pollock's Course of Time," in *Poems and Prose Writings,* vol. 2, 2d ed. (New York: Baker & Scribner, 1850), 351. All subsequent references to this review refer to this edition of *Poems and Prose Writings*.

7. Richard Henry Dana to Richard Henry Dana, Jr., 14 July 1832, Dana Papers, Massachusetts Historical Society.

8. Dana to Sarah Arnold, 28 May 1831, Dana Papers.

9. Dana to Edmund and Richard Henry Dana, Jr., 19 August 1831, Dana Papers.

10. Charles Francis Adams, *Richard Henry Dana: A Biography* (Boston and New York: Houghton Mifflin Co., 1890), 20.

11. Dana, *An Account of the Controversy,* 10.

12. Dana, Jr., *The Journal* 2:608.

13. Dana's reviews published in *Spirit of the Pilgrims* were "Pollock's Course of Time," 1 (October 1828):516–40; "Taylor's Natural History of Enthusiasm," 3 (May, 1830):256–79; and "Martyn's Memoir," 4 (August 1831):428–41. His poems "Thoughts on the Soul" and "Factitious Life" were published in the first edition of his collected work, *Poems and Prose Writings* (Boston: Russell, Odione, & Co., 1833).

14. Dana, "Taylor's Natural History of Enthusiasm," in *Poems and Prose Writings,* vol. 2, 2d ed. (New York: Baker & Scribner, 1850), 388. All

subsequent references to this review refer to this edition of *Poems and Prose Writings*.

15. Ibid., 389.
16. Ibid., 388.
17. Ibid., 389.
18. Dana, "Factitious Life," in *Poems and Prose Writings,* vol. 1, 2d ed. (New York: Baker & Scribner, 1850), 64. All subsequent references to this poem refer to this edition of *Poems and Prose Writings*.
19. Ibid., 73.
20. Dana, "Taylor's Natural History," 2:386.
21. Ibid., 399.
22. Samuel Coleridge's *Aids to Reflection* was originally published in London in 1825. The American edition, which included an important introduction by James Marsh, was published in 1829.
23. Dana, "Factitious Life" 1:81.
24. Dana, "Thoughts on the Soul," in *Poems and Prose Writings,* vol. 1, 2d ed. (New York: Baker & Scribner, 1850), 85.
25. Ibid., 88–89.
26. Dana, "Factitious Life," 1:79.
27. Ibid., 81.
28. Dana to Arnold, 2 March 1838, Dana Papers. Dana's views of transcendentalism are easily inferred from his ironic references in this letter to "higher instincts" and to the belief in the "all sufficiency in ourselves."
29. Arminians believe that the individual plays a part in determining the destiny of his or her soul. The individual is free to accept grace or reject it. Arminians do not believe in the Calvinist doctrine of predestination.
30. Dana, "Taylor's Natural History" 1:392–93.
31. Dana, "Pollock's Course of Time" 2:354.
32. Ibid., 355.
33. Dana to Enoch Pond, November 1828, Dana Papers.
34. Doreen Hunter, "America's First Romantics: Richard Henry Dana, Sr. and Washington Allston," *New England Quarterly* 45 (March 1972):3–30.
35. Washington Allston, *Lectures on Art and Poems,* ed. Richard Henry Dana, Jr. (New York: Baker & Scribner, 1850), 13.
36. Dana, Jr., *The Journal* 1:149.
37. Dana, "Diaries," in *Poems and Prose Writings,* vol. 2, 2d ed. (New York: Baker & Scribner, 1850), 431.
38. Ibid., 437.
39. Ibid., 427.
40. Dana to Bryant, 7 October 1833, Dana Papers.
41. Dana sent his second son Edmund to the University of Vermont. Harvard had become too Unitarian for his tastes.
42. Ronald Wells, *Three Christian Transcendentalists: James Marsh; Caleb*

Sprague Henry; Frederic Henry Hedge (New York: Columbia University Press, 1943), 163. The comment on Emerson is Marsh's.

43. Ibid., 164–65.

44. Dana to Caleb Sprague Henry, 29 April 1838, Dana Papers.

45. Sidney Ahlstrom, *A Religious History*, 623.

46. "Dana's Poems and Prose Writings," *The Christian Register* 12 (September 1833):150.

47. Dana to William Cullen Bryant, 30 September 1833, Dana Papers.

48. Dana to Martha Dana Allston, 24 September 1833, Dana Papers.

49. C. C. Felton, "Dana's Poems and Prose Writings," *Christian Examiner* 15 (1834):392.

50. Ibid., 392–93.

51. Ibid., 403.

52. Ibid., 402.

53. Ibid., 403.

54. Henry Wadsworth Longfellow, "Dana's Poems and Prose Writings," *American Monthly Review* 4 (1833):470.

55. Dana, "Paul Felton," in *Poems and Prose Writings*, vol. 1, 2d ed. (New York: Baker & Scribner, 1850), 316.

56. Nehemiah Adams, "Dana's Poems and Prose Writings," *The Literary and Theological Review* 1 (June 1834):234.

57. Dana to Bryant, 11 June 1834, Dana Papers.

58. Amos Bronson Alcott journals, February 1837, Alcott-Pratt Collection, Houghton Library, Harvard University.

Chapter Six

1. Richard Henry Dana to William Cullen Bryant, August 1838, Dana Papers, Massachusetts Historical Society.

2. Charles Follen, *The Works of Charles Follen*, vol. 1, ed. E. L. Follen (Boston: Hilliard, Gray & Co., 1841), 347.

3. Dana to Ruth Charlotte Dana, 8 October 1834, Dana Papers.

4. Dana to Sarah Arnold, 4 May 1835, Dana Papers.

5. Dana to Bryant, 2 March 1836, Dana Papers.

6. Dana to Arnold, 21 December 1834, Dana Papers.

7. Richard Henry Dana, "Law as Suited to Man," in *Poems and Prose Writings*, vol. 2, 2d ed. (New York: Baker & Scribner, 1850), 73. The lecture was originally published in *Biblical Repository and Quarterly Observer*, 1835.

8. Dana, lecture 2, p. 8, Dana Papers, Massachusetts Historical Society.

9. Ibid., 26.

10. Ibid.

11. Ibid., 27–28.

12. Ibid., 31.
13. Roy Harvey Pearce, *The Continuity of American Poetry* (Princeton, N.J.: Princeton University Press, 1965), 5, 137–41.
14. Dana, "The Past and the Present," in *Poems and Prose Writings* 2:14–49. Originally delivered as a Lyceum lecture. "The Past and The Present" was published in the *American Quarterly Observer*, 1833.
15. Ibid., 38.
16. Ibid., 32.
17. Ibid., 39–40.
18. Ibid., 37.
19. Ibid., 29–30.
20. Excerpt from a letter of Edmund Quincy to Richard D. Webb, 22 September 1844, Dana Papers.
21. Dana, "Law as Suited to Man" 2:58.
22. Ibid., 81.
23. Dana to Arnold, 26 February 1834, Dana Papers.
24. Dana, "Law as Suited to Man" 2:95.
25. Ibid., 81.
26. Ibid., 84.
27. Ibid., 78.
28. Ibid., 94–95.
29. Ibid., 89.
30. Ibid., 96.
31. Dana to Arnold, 21 December 1835, Dana Papers.
32. Ibid., 74.
33. Dana, lecture 1, p. 6, Dana Papers.
34. Ibid., 9, 27.
35. Ibid., 10.
36. Dana, lecture 2, p. 21, Dana Papers.
37. Ibid., 17.
38. Dana, lecture 3, p. 13, Dana Papers.
39. Ibid., 16.
40. Dana, lecture 4, p. 32, Dana Papers.
41. Ibid., 11.
42. Ibid., 12.
43. Dana, lecture 6, p. 4, Dana Papers.
44. Ibid., 14.
45. Dana, lecture 7, p. 15, Dana Papers.
46. Ibid., 18.
47. Ibid.
48. Ibid., 2.
49. Dana, lecture 8, pp. 11–12, Dana Papers.
50. Ibid., 5.
51. Ibid., 17.

52. Ibid., 18.

53. Ibid., 32.

54. This comment was recorded by Richard Henry Dana, Jr., after a particularly inept and comical performance of the play. *The Journal of Richard Henry Dana, Jr.*, vol. 1, ed. Robert F. Lucid (Cambridge: Harvard University Press, Belknap Press, 1968), 291.

55. Ralph Waldo Emerson, *The Letters of Ralph Waldo Emerson*, vol. 2, ed. Ralph L. Rusk (New York and London: Columbia University Press, 1939), 190.

56. Dana to Edmund T. Dana, April 1850, Dana Papers.

57. George W. Peck, "Poems and Prose Writings of Richard H. Dana," *American Whig Review* 2 (January 1850); 66–76. Edwin Percy Whipple, "Dana's Poems and Prose Writings," *Christian Examiner* 48 (1850):247–65.

58. Peck, "Poems and Prose Writings," 67.

59. Ibid.

60. Ibid., 70.

61. Ibid., 73, 74.

62. Dana to Dana, Jr., 26 January 1850, Dana Papers.

63. Whipple, "Dana's Poems and Prose Writings," 253.

64. Ibid., 249.

65. Ibid., 250.

66. Ibid., 251.

67. Ibid., 250.

68. Dana, Jr., *The Journal* 1:304.

69. Dana to Arnold, 5 June 1834, Dana Papers.

70. Dana to Bryant, 14 October 1840, Dana Papers.

Selected Bibliography

Primary Sources

1. Published Works
Poems and Prose Writings. 2 vols. New York: Baker & Scribner, 1850.

2. Manuscripts
Dana's correspondence and a typewritten copy of his "Lectures on Shakespeare" are in the Massachusetts Historical Society. William Cullen Bryant's correspondence provides essential material for piecing together Dana's story. The Bryant materials are located in the Bryant-Godwin Collection and the Goddard-Roslyn Collection at the New York Public Library.

Secondary Sources

Bate, Walter Jackson. *From Classic to Romantic: Premises of Taste in Eighteenth Century England.* Harper Torchbook ed. New York: Harper & Row, 1961. Essential for understanding the transition from neoclassical to romantic literary ideas.

Boller, Paul F. *American Transcendentalism, 1830–1860: An Intellectual Inquiry.* Capricorn Books ed. New York: G. P. Putnam's Sons, 1974. A very useful introduction to the thought of the transcendentalists; helpful to understanding the similarities and differences between Dana's position and that of the transcendentalists.

Brown, Charles H. *William Cullen Bryant.* New York: Charles Scribner's Sons, 1971. Standard biography of Bryant. Fails to do justice to the importance of the friendship between the two men.

Charvat, William. *The Origins of American Critical Thought, 1810–1835.* New York: A. S. Barnes, Perpetua Books, 1961. An appreciative account of Dana's importance as a literary critic and of his pioneering role in introducing Americans to romantic critical ideas.

Dana, Richard H., Jr. *The Journal of Richard Henry Dana, Jr.* Edited by Robert F. Lucid. 3 vols. Cambridge: Harvard University Press, Belknap Press, 1968. Valuable source of information on the relationship between father and son and on the impact that Dana, Sr.'s, troubled life had on his family.

Fogel, Richard. *The Idea of Coleridge's Criticism.* Berkeley and Los Angeles: University of California Press, 1962. Includes an introduction to Coleridge's ideas about the imagination and his theories of literary criticism.

Gale, Robert L. *Richard Henry Dana.* New York: Twayne Publishers, 1969. A solid study of the literary achievement of the younger Dana. Perpetuates old stereotypes about Richard Henry Dana, Sr.

Green, Martin. *The Problem of Boston.* Norton Library ed. New York: W. W. Norton & Co., 1967. Green's book is concerned with the period after Dana's most productive years, but his discussion of the pressures at work forcing writers to conform to a code of gentility helps explain Dana's difficulties and isolation.

————— "The God that Neglected to Come, American Literature 1780–1820." In *American Literature to 1900.* Vol. 8 of *History of Literature in the English Language.* Edited by Marcus Cunliffe. London: Barrie & Jenkins, 1973. Essential background for understanding the problems faced by the writers of Dana's generation.

Howe, Daniel Walker. *The Unitarian Conscience: Harvard Moral Philosophy, 1805–1861.* Cambridge: Harvard University Press, 1970. A superb account of the ideas and attitudes that dominated Harvard and influenced the cultural standard-bearers against whom Dana pitted himself.

Hunter, Doreen M. "America's first Romantics: Richard Henry Dana, Sr. and Washington Allston." The *New England Quarterly* XLV (March 1972):3–30. Stresses the parallels in the careers of Dana and Allston, emphasizing their common doubts about the creative imagination.

Pearce, Roy Harvey. *The Continuity of American Poetry.* Princeton, N.J.: Princeton University Press, 1967. In chapters 4 and 5 of this study of American poetry, Pearce discusses how a number of nineteenth-century poets dealt with the antipoetic quality of America.

Peckham, Morse. *The Triumph of Romanticism: Collected Essays by Morse Peckham.* Columbia: University of South Carolina Press, 1970. Thought-provoking essays on the varieties and progression of literary romanticism.

Wells, Ronald Vale. *Three Christian Transcendentalists: James Marsh, Caleb Sprague Henry, Frederic Henry Hedge.* New York: Columbia University Press, 1943. Describes the ideas of Dana's friends and allies in the movement for a conservative spiritual philosophy.

Index